THE
TROUBLED

AMERICAN

RICHARD LEMON

A CLARION BOOK

PUBLISHED BY SIMON AND SCHUSTER

A CLARION BOOK
PUBLISHED BY SIMON AND SCHUSTER
ROCKEFELLER CENTER, 630 FIFTH AVENUE
NEW YORK, NEW YORK 10020

FIRST CLARION PAPERBACK PRINTING 1971
SBN 671-20694-X CASEBOUND EDITION
SBN 671-21065-3 CLARION PAPERBACK EDITION
LIBRARY OF CONGRESS CATALOG CARD NUMBER: 73-130481
DESIGNED BY CARL WEISS
MANUFACTURED IN THE UNITED STATES OF AMERICA

The author is grateful for permission from several publishers to quote from the following works:

"American Names," from *Ballads and Poems* by Stephen Vincent Benét. Copyright 1931 by Stephen Vincent Benét. Copyright © 1959 by Rosemary Carr Benét. Reprinted by permission of Holt, Rinehart and Winston, Inc.

The Emerging Republican Majority by Kevin P. Phillips. Copyright © 1969 by Arlington House, New Rochelle, New York. Used with permission.

"The Political Discovery of the Year" by Jimmy Breslin, which originally appeared in *New York* Magazine. Used by permission.

"Prairie" from *Cornhuskers* by Carl Sandburg. Copyright 1918 by Holt, Rinehart and Winston, Inc. Copyright 1946 by Carl Sandburg. Reprinted by permission of Holt, Rinehart and Winston, Inc.

Reveille for Radicals by Saul D. Alinsky. Copyright © 1969 by Saul Alinsky. Published by Random House, Inc. Used by permission.

"The Revolt of the White Lower Middle Class" by Pete Hamill. Reprinted by permission of International Famous Agency, Inc. Copyright © 1969 by New York Magazine Company. The full article originally appeared in *New York* Magazine.

"Sources of Public Unhappiness" by Richard Goodwin. Copyright © 1969 by Richard Goodwin. Reprinted by permission of The Sterling Lord Agency. The article originally appeared in *The New Yorker*.

"Politicizing the Lower-middle" by Michael Novak. The article originally appeared in *Commonweal*. Used by permission.

Why Can't They Be Like Us? by Father Andrew M. Greeley, copyright © 1969 by Institute of Human Relations Press. All rights reserved.

CONTENTS

PREFACE

During the spring and summer of 1969, it became increasingly clear to many Americans that something was up in what was then being christened "middle America." Depending on where one stood, there was a rustling in the bushes, or footsteps in the night, or even thunder on the right. There was no shortage of definitions of this ferment, but there was a great lack of agreement: The commentators were often like the blind men who tried to define an elephant by its feel—one felt a leg and pronounced it a tree, and another felt the trunk and declared that it was clearly a snake. There seemed to be a need for a less subjective and random approach to the phenomenon.

To try to get at the sources of middle America's newfound discontent, *Newsweek* magazine in the fall of 1969 commissioned The Gallup Organization to interview 2,165 white adults comprising a cross-section of white America. Included in this total sample were 1,321 white Americans whose incomes ranged from $5,000 to $15,000—representatives of a group which, by itself, comprises about 55 per cent of the U.S. population. While the Gallup pollsters were filling out their questionnaires, Karl Fleming, *Newsweek*'s bureau chief in Los Angeles and a veteran reporter of the civil rights struggle, spent five weeks criss-crossing the United States, talking to used-car salesmen, factory hands, clerks, housewives, and other random representatives of middle America. At the same time, *Newsweek* reporters in Pittsburgh, Boston, Detroit, Chicago, New York, Washington, Minneapolis, Los Angeles, San Francisco, Houston, and Atlanta talked to other middle Americans, and to sociologists, politicians, philosophers, and psychiatrists who have observed and thought about their problems.

The results were published in the October 6 issue of *Newsweek* in five separate articles: One, by National Affairs Editor Edward Kosner, gave an overview of the findings of the pollsters, reporters, and observers; one, by Senior Editor Lawrence S. Martz, gave a detailed look at the poll findings; one, by Karl Fleming, gave sketches of fourteen of the middle Americans he had interviewed; one, by General Editor Kenneth Auchincloss, reported on the new folk heroes of middle America; and one, by *Newsweek* consultant Richard M. Scammon, analyzed the political implications of the new unrest. It was the first major magazine piece to take a hard, close, and detailed look at middle America, and, as of this writing, it is still the most comprehensive.

At this point, while the *Newsweek* editors were turning to a new batch of subjects and a new issue, I collected all the material for the special issue in a large, brown suitcase and went home to write this book. There was a great deal of valuable material for which there had been no room in the magazine. There were also questions raised by the material itself which suggested additional areas for investigation. During the next few months, at my request, The Gallup Organization ran off two books of additional poll data, comparing the answers of sixteen sub-groups in the poll sample: those under thirty who felt the country was in better shape than it used to be, those who had said Negroes had a better chance at a good job than they did, and so on. (Appendix B gives a breakdown of the poll sample by age, political affiliation, etc.) At the same time, many of the reporters in *Newsweek*'s bureaus went back to their original sources for follow-up interviews on specific questions raised by the original material. Finally, three pretty and talented *Newsweek* researchers, Sally Hunter, Susan Fleming, and Pat Conway, supplied additional information, answered all questions that were answerable, and verified all the new material.

All told, close to one hundred people at *Newsweek* have contributed in various ways to the material used in this book. Karl Fleming is responsible for all the material in the vignettes of middle Americans which are scattered throughout the book. The following *Newsweek* correspondents are responsible for most of the rest of the non-poll material: Tom Mathews, in New York; Richard T. Stout and Kendra Heymann, in Washington; Frank W. Morgan, Jr., and Malcolm MacPherson, in Boston; Robert S. Stokes, Merton D. Perry, and Don Holt, in Chicago; Stephan Lesher, in Atlanta; Louis Alexander, *Newsweek*'s stringer in Houston; James C. Jones, Jon Lowell, and William Serrin, in Detroit; John L. Dotson, Jr., in Los Angeles; and Peter Barnes, William J. Cook, and Gerald C. Lubenow, in San Francisco. All these correspondents were coordinated by Senior Editor Rod Gander, who also conceived of and coordinated this book.

My own role as writer of the book can be described simply. From the time I picked up the material until publication, I had a great deal of help and no orders. The form of the book is my doing, and the book's deductions are my deductions, based on the material in hand.

Compared with the traditional formula of one writer/one manuscript, this seems like a queer way of creating a book, but one of the pleasures of journalism and literature is that there are no rules—which is a lucky thing, because a book like this could not have come about in the traditional way.

The book is a product of collaboration, and collaboration has both its virtues and its limitations. There is no way to duplicate the unique insight of a lone reporter who has gone out and collected, first-hand, the stuff he is going to write about. Neither is there any way to duplicate the freedom and variety inherent in the ability to send a cable to twenty cities and have twenty good reporters go out and collect the kind of material you have asked for; each one will collect it in his own way, and will ask questions that neither you nor anybody else would have thought of. Each of these methods has its uses, and one of the great virtues of the bureau system is that it has increased the possible ways in which any given subject can be approached; it has expanded the journalistic repertoire. As a practical matter, I would guess that it would have taken one writer about a year to compile the material in this book, two months to type it all up, three months to collect his thoughts and his breath, and six months to put it all together. I think it would be a fine project, and I would look forward to reading the results in two or three years. In the meantime, thanks to the foresight of the *Newsweek* editors and their ability to tap the varied talents of a great many people all at once, we have had the special *Newsweek* issue and now this book.

Polling also has its pluses and its minuses. A poll is a way of gabbing over the back fence with a whole segment of the population. Like all conversations, it has its limits as a guide to the future: A woman may deplore her husband's alcoholic business lunches, finish hanging up the wash, and go inside to sneak a nip herself. In the same way, 38.6 per cent of the *Newsweek* sample said that they had voted for Richard M. Nixon in 1968, while only 25 per cent said they voted for Humphrey and only 9.3 per cent said they voted for Wallace. Those figures are almost certainly inaccurate, because pollsters know that people tend to say they voted for the winner whether they did or not. Nonetheless, what people claim to think is important, whether they are 100 per cent truthful are not, and they are usually truthful. Appendix C gives the accepted limits of sampling error for various sizes of samples, and no comparisons between groups have been made in this book unless the difference between them was clearly greater than the margin of error.

It seems to me that there is much that is useful and much that is unsatisfactory about this book. Too much is left to be guessed at. There are too many fragmentary explanations and theories from too many people. There is too much raw material of uncertain meaning, and there are too many loose ends. It is an untidy book. This is not a plea for indulgence, however. Middle America is too big and unruly and unstudied to make a really tidy book, and I believe that this untidy one fills a void: So far, it is the only one of its kind we have, and it seems to me both presumptuous and misleading to try to pass it off as definitive when it is in fact a first exploration.

We need more books—many more—about middle America. In the meantime, what is offered is a conglomeration: a lot of poll data, a lot of chances to look in on middle Americans at home and at work, a lot of views about what ails middle America from both residents and outsiders, and an attempt to draw a rudimentary chart of how the land lies now. Some of the poll data makes difficult reading—there are no colorful synonyms for "per cent"—but it offers the only such material I know of, and the careful reader may find many hints and leads in it that have escaped me. The reporting, I think, is excellent, and it offers the flesh and blood which poll statistics cannot provide. The views presented are wide-ranging and provocative; some of them are reassuring, and some of them are alarming.

In putting all this together, I have drawn as clear a picture of middle America as I thought the material allowed, and no clearer. I think the reader will get a better understanding of some of our current problems, and some answers to a few of them; if he comes out with some new questions, that is also to the good. We in America are used to being offered solutions to everything, and I suspect that one of our problems as a nation has been that we leap at solutions before we understand what the trouble is. This book has no solutions in it. I'm perfectly convinced that, right now, nobody has the answers to our most fundamental troubles. But before we can find the right answers to our national ailments, we first have to learn to ask the right questions. I think this book asks some of the right questions.

1

SOMETHING ROTTEN

Something is wrong here. But what is it?

"Seems like we have lost respect for ourselves."
"I really worry about this country, if we don't change our ways and return to religion."
"Things can't get worse. Our dollar is shrinking. I don't feel safe out at night."
"Got myself a gun, and I'll use it, too."
"The welfare people get out of taxes and so do the rich. The middle-class family is just forgotten."
"The niggers are all organized. So are the Mexicans, even the Indians. But who the hell speaks for me?"
"These college rioters should be put in concentration camps."
"The war stinks."
"People don't care for each other any more."

Something is rotten in America. These cries of protest are coming from no underprivileged minority or radical fringe but from the common people next door: a housewife in Missouri, a farmer in South Carolina, a lady postal worker in Pittsburgh, a lumber salesman in California, a foreman in Maryland, a construction worker in San Francisco, a store manager in Indiana, a feed salesman in Iowa, an old lady in Tennessee. And if you travel across the most powerful country at the end of her most prosperous decade, these are the sort of scenes you find:

At three in the afternoon on a dingy side street of Milwaukee, Wisconsin, gig grinder Ray Walczak, 44, walks off his shift at a grimy, old, heavy-machinery factory toward his rusting Buick. Across the street, Father James Groppi and a group of black militants are picketing for more jobs.

"Look at that," Ray Walczak says. "Bastards don't want jobs. If you offered them jobs now, ninety per cent of them would run like hell. They ought to take machine guns and shoot the bastards. Period. I tell you, people on relief get better jobs, got better homes, than I've got. You're better off now not working. The colored people are eating steak, and this Polack bastard is eating chicken.

"Damn right I'm bitter. The Polish race years ago didn't go out and riot and ruin people's property. I've been in the shops since I was sixteen. I worked like a goddam fool. I've been here eighteen years, and if I live to be a hundred I'll probably be doing the same job. The only raise I ever got was a union raise. I've begged and argued with the bosses, 'I'm not asking for a quarter, just a nickel.' But never a merit raise. They say, 'Be patient, be patient.' They ought to give you a medal for patience. Day after day, year after year, climbing these same steps, punching that time card. Standing in that same goddam spot grinding those same goddam holes. It gets sickening. But they don't care. We're just peons, just numbers. And if you don't like it, there's always somebody waiting for your job."

In a little park in Hammond, Indiana, Fred Huff, truck driver, 41, is spending the day at the lake with his wife and four of his children. At home, in the rented lower half of a peeling frame house, the Huff's oldest son is 80 per cent disabled from mortar wounds received in Vietnam.

"We're luckier than some," Fred Huff says. "At least we got him back alive. I guess I'm more for the war than against it. When some country is threatening your way of life, it has to be stopped somewhere. But I don't know. It's bad enough to lose all these boys. But for something that's pointless? No. I'm afraid it's gonna be another Korea."

Huff looks across Wolf Lake; on either side, a militaristic row of steel mills and an oil refinery are firing salvos of noxious smoke into the sky, and green slime and yellow foam float lazily along the shore.

"Everything is getting uglier and uglier," Fred Huff says. "We don't like a thing here—it's just the money place to be. The steel mills and the refineries make the air so bad it smarts the old eyeballs and makes you nauseated. It's having an effect. People get irritated now over things they would have laughed at years ago. There's a lack of friendliness, no closeness. Half the time you don't even know who your neighbor is, unless there's a fight. Something seems to have gone out of people. Girls are flipping around showing as much as they can."

He looks around the crowded, narrow beach. "Life is getting faster and furiouser," he says. "Sometimes you feel like throwing up your hands and saying to hell with it and going so far back in the hills they'll have to pipe sunshine in. But we've got only a few more years to contend with it. That's why we rent—so when we're ready, all we have to do is pack and tell the kids goodbye. Then Mama and I will bum around out West until we find a place. There's still a lot of beautiful country left."

In the office of the semiweekly *Sunland and Tajunga Record-Ledger* in the foothills of the Verdugo Mountains outside of Los Angeles, editor Ray Brooks, balding and robust, sits at his cluttered desk in his shirt sleeves, a pair of glasses in each shirt pocket, and shakes his head.

"We just seem to be headed toward a collapse of everything," Ray Brooks says. "I'm upset about the kids and the hippies and the absolute disregard for law and order and any kind of convention. It isn't the clothes. Hell, when I was a kid, I wore bell-bottom pants to school with purple balls on the side. But when I was the age of these hippies, I couldn't wait to get out and get a piece of capitalism and become part of the Establishment. But these kids grow up and they don't want to be a part of it. That's what makes people mad. To these kids, the future is nothing. To us, it was everything. It's sad. It's very sad."

He looks helplessly at the floor. "Most Americans have a deep love for their country," he says. "But nowadays they see pollution—the befouling of streams, the air, the parks, our morals, our literature, our music. Everything seems to be dirty and indecent. I'm just happy I'm sixty-three and don't have to go through much more of it."

Meanwhile, in a drug store down the street, Chuck Booth —26, tanned, muscular, a salesman out in the Golden West —drinks Coke from a bottle and sticks out a powerful hand.

"Look at my fingernails," Chuck Booth says, pointing to raw, red stubs. "I'm uptight and afraid of the future, and nine out of ten people I talk to are uptight. I'd like to get married and have a family, but I'm not sure I'm emotionally capable of handling that right now."

What is going on here in the land of the free and the home of the brave, the last, best hope of mankind? What can have happened to these everyday folks who make up more than half of the richest and freest nation in the world? In other times, through all grumblings and dissensions, there were always proud voices boasting of the spirit of the people. "We are not a narrow tribe of men," Herman Melville wrote. "The fabulous country—the place where miracles not only happen, but where they happen all the time," wrote Thomas Wolfe. "The people—yes," wrote Carl Sandburg. There are few proud voices now, and nobody is saying yes to the people any more.

The people themselves suddenly seem to be consumed

with an aimless, puzzled, pervasive discontent. Sometimes they are angry. "All the government wants from us is our money and our boys to send to Vietnam," says a mother of six in Minneapolis. "They don't give a cotton picking gol-darn about anything else." Sometimes they are querulous and self-pitying. "Why," explodes a plumber in Los Angeles, "I can't even afford a color-TV set!" Sometimes they talk sadly of beliefs that are passing. "Ten years ago, you had a sense of values," says a secretary in Tacoma, Washington. "You knew what tomorrow would bring. Today you don't. There's no security." Sometimes they talk about needing a good dictator. "We should have a Hitler here to get rid of the troublemakers, the way they did with the Jews in Ger-many," says a house repairman in California. Often they say they don't know who to turn to, or where the way out lies. "Where does it all stop?" asks an insurance broker in Pittsburgh. "That's what people ask. Who can give us the answers to these things?" And most often of all, they pass a frightening judgment: They say that what is wrong is not just this or that but the whole country, everybody, every-thing. "Everything is dirty and indecent." "Everything is getting uglier and uglier." "We just seem to be headed to-ward a collapse of everything."

Something is very wrong here, The question is, has some-thing gone wrong, or was something wrong all along?

2

THE TROUBLED AMERICANS

There seemed to be no end to the trouble in paradise. In the last years of the 1960's, America was rich beyond even her cocky expectations, yet discontent seemed to be spreading like some new, elusive plague of the age of technology. In a country proud of its big appetite, there suddenly seemed to be too much of everything: too many people, too many factories, too much pollution, too many cars, too many taxes, too much crime, too many strikes, too much war, too much discord, too much change. As though answering some roll call of the dispossessed, group after group had risen up during the decade to declare its grievances and, often, to flaunt its defiance to the established ways. When Richard M. Nixon became the 37th President, he seemed about to cry a halt to all that. He seemed to offer the reassurance that the decade's discords had been warped out of all proportion, and he called on something named "the silent majority" to come forth and show the world that all was really as it had always been—that men worked, women cooked, children obeyed, pleasures were innocent, days were purposeful, nights were quiet, and life made sense. He would seek out these forgotten, orderly men and women, and the squabbles of the past would fall into perspective, because the people had had enough of them. And then, when these common men were invited to come forward and speak, it turned out that they were full of grievances, too, that they had had enough in ways they could only partly define, and that the great middle class of America was as eroded with discontent as all the rest.

After a decade in which the nation's attention has been fixed on minorities, politicians, reporters and sociologists have rediscovered the great American middle class, but the words being used to describe it are new and disconcerting: "alienated," "frightened," "uneasy," "forlorn," "angry," "resentful," "confused." It is as though the old view of the common man had been stood on its ear, and the people whom Andrew Jackson called "the bone and sinew of the country" had been transformed into a bewildered, sullen, and splintered majority. They have the numbers to run things their own way, but they don't seem to know, or be able to agree on, what their own way is. Sometimes they are said to be on the edge of revolt. "You better watch out," thunders Eric Hoffer, the longshoreman-philosopher. "The common man is standing up and someday he's going to elect a policeman President of the United States." Sometimes they are said to be on the verge of surrender. "More and more people are recognizing that there is so little they can do to improve their situation that they are simply giving up," says Dr. Jarl Dryud, Director of Clinical Services at the University of Chicago. "I don't think I've ever seen this country so apathetic." But whether they are rising in anger or sinking in despair, the middle Americans, in the sour words of their President, are clearly "fed up to here."

The exact nature of this middle American malaise, and the expression it finds, will affect the course of the country throughout the 1970's. "Let's face it," says Saul Alinsky, the 61-year-old dean of American radicals. "The middle class represents four-fifths of this country's population. If you took every minority group in this country and somehow got them together, they still wouldn't have the numbers to change things. The middle class has the numbers, but they feel too cut off from the entire society to change things. Someone has got to show them how to get a voice in this country."

The truth of this observation has not been lost on the country's sociologists or its politicians. The Ford Foundation is now financing studies of middle America, and the Harvard-M.I.T. Joint Center for Urban Studies has taken the middle Americans as its main subject for study in 1970. Robert Wood, its director and Under Secretary of Housing and Urban Development under President Johnson, worries about whether the unrest is economic, and therefore solvable, or ethnic, and thus explosive.

The new interest in middle America also crosses all political lines. Joseph Duffey, National Chairman of the liberal Americans for Democratic Action and the son of a West Virginia coal miner, has said, "It seems to me it is crucial that there emerge in this country a new populism which can be an expression of anger and indignation at the problems of those people who still live in great economic and social insecurity, and even in new affluence struggle to make ends meet." Senator Fred Harris, former Chairman of the Democratic National Committee, has talked of forging a "new populism" of the poor and the middle class. The President of the United States claims the middle Americans for his silent majority. "These are my people," he says. "We speak the same language." And Vice President Spiro T. Agnew, lashing out at protesters and the press, is paying the most open attention of all. "Agnew is reading middle income America better than any other man on the political scene," says Roman Pucinski, a Democratic Representative from Chicago, and even some black leaders are urging that closer attention be paid to what Agnew says. "Agnew is saying publicly what a lot of people say when they sit beside you on an airplane," Clarence Mitchell, President of the Washington, D.C., bureau of the NAACP, has said. "It's very important for us to listen carefully, because I think he's reflecting a widely held point of view."

The picture of middle Americans painted by the *Newsweek* reports is one of deep alienation from a social system which, by rights, they ought to dominate. They feel that their country has lost its way, and that it may well get worse still in the years ahead. They are alarmed about Vietnam: It seems to them that America was justified in going in there, but they tend to think we would have done better to stay out—and they want it ended somehow. They are upset about the cost of everything, and they don't feel they're getting as big a share as they deserve. They think the country has lost its sense of values. They are appalled at the nudity and sex on display in movies, magazines, and books, and they think the people are turning away from religion. Neither neighbors nor strangers seem as friendly as they used to. They think the old rules have been changed unfairly. They concede that Negroes have some legitimate complaints, but say they are asking for too much, too fast. They believe that the Negro is getting special favors, at least in certain areas, and that the danger of racial violence is increasing.

They think that black militants and college demonstrators are getting away with murder, that the cops don't have enough power and that judges ought to be able to lock up accused criminals without bail before trial. They think the people on welfare are getting something for nothing and could work if they wanted to. They are skeptical of what politicians and their news sources tell them, and they don't think their tax money is being used right: They say too much is wasted on space programs and foreign aid, and not enough spent on pollution, job training, and crime—the problems close to home. They simply don't like the way things are heading for their country or themselves, and they don't feel that they have anything to say about it.

"People seemed almost pathetically eager to talk, as if

Q. WHAT DO YOU THINK ARE THE MOST IMPORTANT PROBLEMS FACING THE NATION?

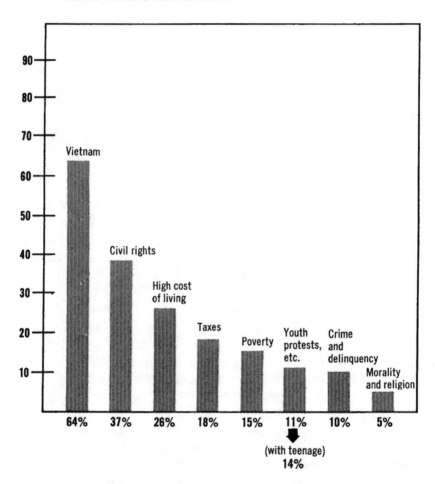

nobody had ever asked before," Karl Fleming wrote of his trip through middle America, "and almost universally they were in a fretful, fearful, disquieted mood. They were irritable and uneasy—about high taxes, welfare, high prices, and pollution—and they feel threatened by a terrifying array of enemies: hippies, Black Panthers, dirty books and movies, drugs, the sexually liberated, people who question the sanctity of marriage and the morality of work. They are hostile toward poor and rich alike—toward the poor for being on welfare, toward the rich for not paying taxes—and they are increasingly cynical about politicians. What people seem to want above all else is order: if everybody would just quiet down and quit threatening to destroy what they have worked so hard to build and preserve."

Signs of a resurgence in middle America are everywhere. Coast to coast, cars blossom with decals of the American flag and bumper stickers reading "America—Love It or Leave It." There are movements to get prayers back in the public schools and sex education out of them. There are campaigns to restore law and order and decency. Policemen have been elected Mayors in Detroit and Minneapolis. School bond issues have been rejected from Long Island to California, and bills have been introduced in state and national legislatures to curb campus unrest and insure propriety. In Los Angeles, briefly, there was even a law prohibiting those over 21 from dancing with those under 21, although it was never clear which group the law was designed to protect.

But there are no bumper stickers to express apathy, and the middle American is disheartened at least as often as he is angry. "Generally, there has been a turning away from everything and everyone by the middle class," says Saul Alinsky, who has turned from organizing minority groups to organizing the masses. "They have a feeling of being lost, a feeling that there is no one to turn to, a feeling they don't have anyone to speak for them. The white middle class is suffering from mass schizophrenia. You always hear the expression 'not getting involved.' "

Noting both the anger and the discouragement, some observers have painted the middle American as a man veering toward the political right, hostile toward the black man, ready to rise up and smite his tormentors or to vote for somebody who will. "Everybody wants a gun," says a community worker in a Slavic section of Milwaukee. "They think they've heard from black power, wait till they hear from white power—the little slob, GI Joe, the guy who breaks his ass and makes the country go. Boy, he's getting sick and tired of all the mess. One day he'll get fed up, and when he does, look out!"

The *Newsweek* poll suggests that such a portrait is a caricature. The fact is, everybody doesn't want a gun enough to get one: In the poll, fewer than 4 per cent of those interviewed said they had bought a gun because of their fears. GI Joe fought his war 25 years ago, and he is now pushing or past 50. He is clearly sick and tired of all this mess, but he doesn't yet know the way out.

Moreover, the elections of 1969 did not bear out predictions of a rightward swing. Some law and order candidates won, but most of the more blatant ones lost. In city after city, the appeal of candidates, whose ears get as close to the ground as anybody's, was muted and carefully non-inflammatory. In Pittsburgh, where demonstrations by white construction workers against Negro job demands had almost erupted in violence, the more liberal candidate won. In Boston, Mrs. Louise Day Hicks, whose crusade against the busing of black children had made her a heroine of the right, rolled up by far the biggest vote of eighteen candidates for the City Council—but the second biggest vote-getter was a Negro, and many people voted for both of them.

Politically the middle American has so far swung neither left nor right, and the shadings within middle America make it difficult for consistent coalitions to form. The middle Americans are not a monolithic group, and they are divided by income, age, occupation, level of education, ethnic background, and even political philosophy. The melting pot has not worked very well and foreign-born Americans have assimilated much less than they thought, but even with increasing black demands and white resistance, there is less racial bloodshed than ever before.

One of the largest groupings within middle America is the ethnic groups collectively, if ungrammatically, known as "the ethnics." In the U. S. today, 24 million Americans, or 13 per cent of the population, have at least one foreign-born parent, and nine million more were foreign-born themselves. "Any politician who doesn't pay attention to 40 million ethnics is a fool," Leon Shull, national director of the ADA, has said, and the ADA is currently working to keep the ethnic groups within the Democratic coalition. "Right now, the ethnic vote is up for grabs," says Paul Deac, executive vice president of the National Confederation of American Ethnic Groups in Washington.

But grabbing the ethnic vote is not an easy matter, because "the ethnics" are not one group. "It would make our job easier if we could appeal to the nationality groups as one bloc, but it is impossible," Andrew Valuchek of the Democratic National Committee has said. "They have their own problems and their own lives, and they hate the thought of having their lives disturbed. We have to appeal to each group individually."

The *Newsweek* poll pointed up other divisions. When the middle Americans were asked whether they felt more or less confident about the country's ability to solve its problems than they had five years ago, they were evenly divided —40 per cent more confident, 40 per cent less confident. But 45 per cent of those under 30 felt more confident, while only 30 per cent of those over 55 felt more confident, and 49 per cent felt less confident. Of those in white collar jobs, 47 per cent were more confident, while only 37 per cent of the blue collar workers felt more confident. Education level produced the biggest split of all. A majority of the college educated felt more confidence in the country, and fewer than a third felt less confidence, while a majority of those who had not gone past grade school were less confident, and only a fourth were more confident.

This same line-up materialized on many questions in the poll: the young, the educated, and the white collar versus the old, the under-educated, and the blue collar. Yet these groups are phantom coalitions, because few organizations are based on the factors involved. Instead age, income, education and occupation tend to fragment groups and organizations that do exist. Education often produced bigger splits than income alone, so that the under-educated reacted differently from the well educated, regardless of income. Blue collar workers reacted differently from white collar workers who were earning the same amount of money. Income alone created certain differences. Those at the lower end of the economic spectrum have a shaky hold on middle income status, while those at the upper end are close to qualifying as affluent, and they define their problems a little differently. But income alone was often less decisive than other factors.

Middle America, therefore, is a politically and philosophically varied place, and the one thread that ties all its groups together is resentment. The middle Americans are too fragmented to form an effective coalition, but their impotence does not ease their frustrations. They have somewhat different bills of particulars, but their basic charge against society is the same: they do not like it, they do not feel proud of it, and they often do not feel a part of it. The real question for America is not whether the middle Americans can force a change but whether they are right and, if they are, whether America's institutions will pay heed and adjust themselves.

To do that, it is necessary to distinguish between the quality of the middle American's concerns and the noise he makes. The middle Americans speak with many voices, from shouts to whispers. In the commotion of the twentieth century, it is easy to hear only the shouts and conclude that an uprising is underway. But noise level is not the only measure of discontent, and in middle America it seems to be a fairly unreliable one. The middle American's discontent today seems to be less virulent, more widespread, and more complex than his slogans suggest, and it also seems to be different from other popular outcries of the past.

It is the fond delusion of each younger generation that nobody ever had so much trouble to correct, and of each older generation that nobody ever had so much discontent to control, and there is no good evidence that any generation was really right. The quarrels which rack America today sometimes seem to be signs that the nation is coming apart, but divisiveness is a thoroughly American condition. As a nation, America was conceived in quarrels. More than half the people of New York State were loyal to the King of England. George Washington's army was raggedly clothed and wretchedly housed, because he could not get contributions of materials from his countrymen, and his volunteer army was never up to its quotas because young men chose to fight only when their own community was threatened, and sometimes not at all.

Like every other nation, America's past is drenched in violence. On May 16, 1691, on the site of New York's City Hall Park, Jacob Leisler, a patriot and the duly appointed head of the state militia, was captured by the British and hanged by his countrymen, who cut him down while he was still alive, ripped out his bowels and burned them before his face, cut off his head, quartered him, and paraded bits of his hair and clothing through the streets. The country celebrated its 85th birthday with a bloody civil war. It has seen riots and despots in every age, and each new group of immigrants has been fought by each preceding one. Its people have plundered the land ever since they set foot on it: the forests of Maine were laid bare one hundred and fifty years ago, and California's hills and valleys and rivers were despoiled in the search for gold 120 years ago. There have been bread lines within forty years, union riots within thirty, witch hunts within twenty. There is nothing that seems wrong with the country today that does not have a long and generally much more gruesome heritage behind it.

What makes the current discontent unusual is not its existence but its uncertainty and its pervasiveness in a time of unequaled prosperity and even, despite Vietnam, peacefulness. Americans, though not as well off as they think they are, are better off than anybody has ever been before. For the middle Americans, including those at the lower end of the economic spectrum, life is not a struggle to get food and shelter but to get a few more amenities.

Moreover, except possibly for government programs for the Negro and welfare recipients, there is not an important domestic governmental policy of the last two decades that is under serious attack by any large segment of the population, and even with the Negroes and the welfare program, the middle American has no alternate policy to offer. The original Populist movement of the 1890's had a target—the Wall Street manipulators—and a policy—silver, not gold. If today's middle Americans are forming a New Populism, it is a movement which so far has neither a target nor a goal.

What seems to be going on in middle America today is not so much a revolt as an agonizing reappraisal. The white American is upset about the quality of life in America.

"America is the only idealistic country in the world," Woodrow Wilson said, and it has had many hot debates about the quality of life. It was founded out of concern for the quality of the religious life, and its civil war was fought over the quality of life created by the institution of slavery. Other issues have pitched group against group over spiritual intangibles throughout American history.

Yet in the decade of the sixties, American life has undergone a social revolution which is unique for its breadth and radicalness, and there has been only scattered resistance. If anybody in 1960 had predicted that in ten years time dresses would hit an all-time high, blouses would become transparent, movies would show nudity and copulation, many young people would take to protest and a few to group living, executives would wear hair over their ears, popular entertainers would wear hair down to their shoulders, popular music would sing of sex and drugs, marijuana would become a campus commonplace, abortion would be legalized, students would lock up their college presidents and get away with it, half a million people would go to Washington to protest a war, black people would riot in northern cities, a national commission would admit to racism, the country's most famous quarterback would wear a mink coat, and a newspaper named *Screw* would be available on newsstands —if anybody ten years ago had said these things were about to befall, he would not have found a respectful listener in the country. Yet these things have taken place, and there has been no sizeable protest. While they were happening, middle America was only shaking its head.

If no protest ever materialized, the only conclusion could be that the entire country had been radicalized in a decade, and the reaction is surfacing now. Some of it is virulent.

"If a bunch of good ol' briarhopper [transplanted Southerners] Ku Kluxers had got ahold of Martin Luther King, he wouldn't have lived as long as he did," says a steelworker in Ohio.

"I think Fulbright should be shot as a traitor, and he would be in any other country except our permissive one," says a retired major in Alabama.

"I'm now receiving the most threatening and meanest letters I've received since the days of Joe McCarthy," Senator Fulbright said late in 1969.

"[We] are especially disgusted with ultra-liberal attitudes advanced by platitude-spouting jelly belly, watery-eyed, hand-wringing political prostitutes, who would subordinate individual and property rights, simply to pacify the demands of an infinitesimal number of weirdos, lobbyists, and extreme militants," an insurance broker in Stamford, Connecticut, wrote *Newsweek*.

But more of the reaction seems to be a positive yearning to get back to simpler times and an old moral code, and it is tempered by some unsettling suspicions—that simpler times are not coming back, that many other people have tossed out the old codes, and most unsettling of all, that the old goals may not have been quite as good as they once seemed. "People are saying 'Everything I learned no longer makes sense,' " Dr. Abraham Kaplan of the University of Michigan says.

"While we seem to have found the good life, we also seem to have lost ourselves," Saul Alinsky has written in his book *Reveille for Radicals,* first published in 1945 and recently revised. "We should be happy, but we are in fact confused, frustrated, resentful, and frightened of the feeling of an ever-growing loneliness. We don't know what to do because we don't know what's wrong, except that we know that something very fundamental is wrong; something is missing which we know is more important than many of the things we have achieved. That something is a sense of ourselves as individuals, as people, as members of the human family. What is at stake is our sanity. Our world is so fractured in every area and at every level that all the different pieces, seemingly so important in themselves, swirl and beat upon us so that we no longer know what anything means."

The middle American's uncertainty has been compounded by the knowledge that things are going wrong in a very concrete way. Alinsky describes the middle American as suffering from a kind of "crisis" crisis. "Every time you turn around, there's a crisis of some sort," he said in a recent interview. "You have the black crisis, the urban crisis —it's just one goddam crisis after another. Besides the crises, you've got gaps: generation gaps, credibility gaps, everyone's got a gap. Air pollution, water pollution, there's always something else to worry about. It's just too much for the average middle class Joe to take. But the worst thing for the middle class is that they feel powerless to do anything about anything."

"I think they feel betrayed," says Paul Jacobs, the writer and a former union organizer. "The work ethic, the notion of work that they have been brought up to deify, is being undermined by the young people. The hippies, Woodstock, all those broads walking around with their tits bouncing. Not only do young people do it, but the media seem to approve it, and the upper class does it, too. In the city, especially in New York, the subways, the telephones, the electricity, the garbage and snow removal, the very quality of life is breaking down. Everything in society that they have been taught is valuable and dependable is breaking down."

In this landscape of shifting values, the middle American is faced with such an array of disrupters that he has trouble singling out his main target. Furthermore, many of the disruptions he dislikes have taken place on the periphery of his own world, and they have been brought to him by television, newspapers, and magazines, which is one reason he is annoyed at television, newspapers, and magazines. As a result, he is more than a bit bewildered as to what is happening, why it is happening, and who is making it happen. "The middle class person is only awaiting the personal, rather than the second-hand, punch in the face before he comes out roaring," one man wrote *Newsweek*.

But the personal punch in the face may never come. John Roche, the Brandeis University historian who served as President Johnson's resident intellectual, believes that President Nixon has already blunted the chances of a direct confrontation between black and white or left and right by serving notice that the sort of demonstrations which could lead to a confrontation will not be tolerated. "The edge is already off," Roche says, "because the election of Nixon put into office people who are not going to be responsible for demonstrations. There will be no great riots—you don't riot against your enemies but against your friends, because you know your friends won't shoot. [Attorney General John] Mitchell means business."

Until and unless the personal punch in the face does

come, however, the middle Americans are left with divided feelings about their tormentors. On question after question in the *Newsweek* poll, their resentment against different groups and developments was undercut by the admission that the groups had some justice and the developments made some sense—that they were mixed curses.

The poll revealed an astonishingly widespread conviction that the Negro, however he may have been discriminated against in the past, is now getting special treatment. In one of the poll's most startling results, a clear plurality of the middle Americans declared that the black man now stood a better chance than they themselves of getting a good job, a good education, decent housing, and unemployment assistance from the government. At the same time, 55 per cent of the middle Americans thought the Negro could have done something about his high unemployment rate, and 73 per cent thought that he could have done something about his slums. And they were alarmed at Negro tactics which, in their view, could lead to violence and bloodshed. They put civil rights second on their list of national problems, and 58 per cent saw the danger of racial violence increasing. A majority of middle Americans thus saw the Negro as a man who, without helping himself, was getting special favors at their expense, and threatening their safety with his demands.

"I see the Negro stepping on my rights," said a finance manager in Los Angeles. "He is asking for more than is justifiably his."

"It looks like whites don't have the rights that Negroes do," said an oil field worker in Texas.

"The more we give them, the more they want," said a young woman in Illinois. "Finally they'll take over."

"They want more than we have," said a housewife in West Covina, California. "They think white people should just lay down and get kicked around."

"They are given jobs by good companies and they don't work," said a policeman in New York. "The backers of the

Negro are making them think that we owe them jobs, and we owe them housing, food, money, for nothing."

It is the notion of something for nothing that most galls the middle American, and that is what he thinks (or claims to think) the Negro is getting. It is also the notion of something for nothing that sticks in his throat when he considers welfare recipients. In the *Newsweek* poll, 79 per cent of all middle Americans said that about half or most of the people getting welfare could earn their own way if they wanted to, and when the middle American thinks of welfare recipients, he tends to think of Negroes.

In the same way, many middle Americans think of crime in terms of black people, and of law and order as a means of controlling them. "What does law and order mean?" an investment advisor in King of Prussia, Pennsylvania, was asked. "Get the niggers," he said. "Nothing else." Almost two-thirds of the middle Americans said that the police have too little power, and slightly more than two-thirds said that judges should be able to deny bail to suspected criminals before their trial.

Seeing himself beleaguered while the Negro gets favors, the middle American does not take kindly to charges that he is a racist, and the celebrated use of that word in the Kerner Report may have stirred up resentments as often as it cleared the air.

"While liberals have accepted the Kerner Report's fundamental conclusion that white racism is a national sickness," Murray Friedman of the American Jewish Committee has written, "it may be that there are some dangers in this kind of approach. A strategy which constantly rubs the nose of the white ethnic group into the ground and keeps saying 'You're guilty, you're guilty, you're guilty,' could quickly produce only diminishing returns. It may, in fact, ultimately be a no-win strategy with regard to many elements of the white population."

"We are told we have to feel guilty!" Eric Hoffer roars. "We've been poor all our lives, and now we're being preached to by every son of a bitch who comes along. The ethnics are discovering that you can't trust those *Mayflower* boys."

In fact, for all his fury against what he sees as favoritism toward blacks, the middle American is in an emotional bind: He is basically sympathetic to black aspirations. In the *Newsweek* poll, almost seven out of ten middle Americans said that at least some black demands were justified, although it will take some time to meet them.

When he turns to the subject of today's young people, the middle American shows many of the same attitudes he does toward the Negro—and winds up in the same quandary. The middle Americans are deeply offended by the behavior of some young people and by the conviction that young protestors are getting away with something. "When I was a kid," the owner of a small restaurant in San Francisco told a *Newsweek* reporter, "if I smarted off to a teacher, I got whipped and sent home. And when I got home, I got whipped again. Nowadays they let the kids do anything they want."

"It's high time we stood up and said to these kids, 'We've come through ten thousand years of civilization and have proven that certain standards keep society going,'" a hospital controller told a Lions Club meeting in Inglewood, California. "So until they come up with something better, they have to live by the rules."

It is almost impossible to overstate the resentment in middle America against the recent turbulence on the nation's college campuses. Almost three out of five in the *Newsweek* poll said that college demonstrators had little or no justification for their actions, and two poll questions regarding the treatment of college demonstrators and black militants yielded, significantly, almost identical results: 84 per cent said that campus demonstrators had been treated too leniently, and 85 per cent said that black militants had been treated too leniently. The anger against college demonstrators has a special spice for those in the lower economic brackets. They resent what they see as ingratitude and irresponsibility on the part of those who have a chance they never got. Moreover, Dr. Abraham Kaplan, a philosophy professor at the University of Michigan, has said the demonstrators "upset their image of what college is—a place where there are trees, where the kids drink cocoa, eat marshmallows, read Shakespeare, and once in the spring the boys can look at the girls' underthings." When some of the kids announce that they are giving up cocoa for pot, and then demand a voice in the running of the college, they are launching a frontal attack on the authority middle America respects and the ideals it has always nurtured. When the authority gives in, or, in the case of the police, is criticized for cracking down, it seems one more piece of evidence that the whole social fabric is coming unwoven.

Yet when the middle American is all done sounding off about the spoiled college kids, he is not completely out of sympathy with their aspirations, either. It may be that his anger has a special poignancy because, in his heart of hearts, he secretly wants to do just what the demonstrators are doing, but what his own morality and training won't permit him. In the *Newsweek* poll, 54 per cent of the middle Americans said that young people were not unduly critical of their country, and that criticism is needed. They may have been declaring that most young people behave themselves and only a few make trouble; in another poll question, 58 per cent said they had a favorable opinion of today's young people. But they may also have been reiterating their belief, which the demonstrators share, that the whole system has gone wrong.

"On the surface, they disapprove of the kids with long hair because of their undisciplined way of life," Dr. Jarl Dryud says. "Unconsciously, they admire the hippies for doing what they would like to do—leave responsibilities behind and be a free spirit."

The Vietnam war, in many ways, poses the biggest dilemma of all. It is not being fought according to the rules, and the middle American thinks it should be, and yet he can't say just how. He wants the war won, but not widened. He wants the war ended, but he has no idea how that can be brought about. He is angry at those who protest against it, yet he himself is not sure that it is all worthwhile. In the *Newsweek* poll, 77 per cent said that the U. S. had at least some reasons for going into Vietnam in the first place, but 70 per cent said that it was a mistake, whether they thought we had reasons or not. Nearly two out of three cited the war as one of America's top problems, and among those who rated President Nixon most highly, the most common reason was that he was working for peace. And the war did not seem to be going well: only 8 per cent believed that the Americans and South Vietnamese were winning, while 20 per cent thought we were losing, and two-thirds thought we were simply holding our own.

The doves and the hawks were both minorities in the poll. Only 19 per cent said that America had "no right or reason" to be in Vietnam, while only 26 per cent said that the country had a "right and duty" to fight the communists. In between these two extremes, 32 per cent said that, although we were justified, it would have been better if we had sent only military aid and supplies, and 19 per cent said that although we had some reasons for going, we should have "stayed out." Nor was there any agreement on what the country should do from now on. About 7 per cent said the U. S. should get out or go all out. Another 11 per cent said the U. S. needed more aggressiveness, and 3 per cent said we should have bombed North Vietnam more. "I can't figure it out," said a retired sand and gravel dealer in Fort Laramie, Ohio. "If you can't go into North Vietnam, what's the use of fighting? If you hit me and go into the next room and I can't follow, what the hell's the use?" "Don't bomb here, don't bomb there—it's a cuddly war," said a nurse in New Jersey. "They should blast them all and come home." The dovish opinions were almost as common, but more pallid, and there were surprisingly few moral arguments against the war. "I can't remember when we started fighting over there," said a 22-year-old restaurant manager in Florida, "but I do think we should have been out long ago."

The war is not an abstraction to the middle Americans. Fifty-five per cent said they personally knew somebody who had been killed or wounded in Vietnam. Its aggravations are not in terms of morality but in terms of costs, both in money and in lives.

"Nothing has them more depressed," Representative Roman Pucinski says of the people in his Chicago district. "Vietnam, the draft have a great impact on over-all happiness. It's a cloud. It takes the pleasure out of good times, the two cars, the new furniture, the home. They come up to me and say, 'Congressman, I finally worked my way up'— and then they mention their boy's going to Vietnam. There's a big pacifist drive. It's getting harder and harder to stir them in defense of great national causes. Most are saying 'Live and let live.' They hope if they hope hard enough, it'll go away."

"The war contributes to the frustration of the middle class," Dr. Dryud says, "because they see it as the ultimate exercise in futility. It's evidence that people are spending their money and not getting anything in return." The anti-war demonstrations only seem to fuel this frustration. John Roche says that the middle Americans see such demonstrations as still another betrayal.

"By and large, the people feel the main thing about the war—and it's true about the Negro situation, too—is that the sacrifices made aren't appreciated," he says." It's the stab-in-the-back theory. They're not concerned about the war as much as the lack of support for it."

The middle American's anger and frustration over Negroes, welfare recipients, crime, the young, and Vietnam are compounded by the fact that, most of the time, he has formed his opinion on second-hand evidence. Even after a dozen years of civil rights activism, most middle Americans do not live or work beside a black man. They seem no more familiar with welfare recipients or criminals. When they were handed a list of problems facing people who live in cities and were asked to pick the two or three most serious, almost two-thirds checked "crimes of violence," and people in the suburbs listed it more often than did actual city dwellers. Yet when they were asked how serious a problem violent crime was in their own communities, 42 per cent said fairly or very serious, and 56 per cent said not too serious or not serious at all. In the same way, 42 per cent checked off welfare as one of the two or three most serious problems facing people in the cities. But when they were asked to list the two or three most important problems in their own communities, an infinitesimal 3 per cent put down "welfare."

For the middle American, therefore, many of the ructions he resents are taking place somewhere else. The crime wave he abhors takes place, he thinks, outside his community. The welfare chiselers are doing their sponging, he believes, in some other town. The fractious kids he would like to wallop belong, he believes, to somebody else. The war he worries about is being fought halfway around the world, although its effects are coming closer to home all the time. Negro demands affect him more directly. He feels that the value of his home, and his children's education, are threatened by them. But the one issue that truly hits home, that is with him every day of the year, is the issue of money. And the middle American doesn't feel that he has as much of it as he deserves.

Americans have always been noted for their high regard for money. There is no equivalent expression in other tongues for "the almighty dollar," and through the years writers have attacked materialism as the original American sin. Materialism is still at the heart of many of the objections of the radical young, and materialism is the most consistent theme of American advertising.

Many middle Americans see very little wrong with that. "Some people say that this country has become too materialistic and interested in making money," they were asked on one question. "Others say people are right in wanting to make as much money as they can. Which side do you agree with more?" A majority of 51 per cent said that people were right in wanting to make as much as they can, and a sizeable minority of 44 per cent said that the country was too materialistic. Such philosophical considerations aside, the middle Americans were clearly disturbed over the amount of money they had in the bank, and the amount of goods that their money would bring them. When they were asked to list the nation's most important problems, the high cost of living came in third and taxes fourth, behind Vietnam and civil rights. When they were asked to list the most important problems in their own community, high taxes came in first, and inflation came in second. When they were asked whether their local taxes were too high, 59 per cent said yes, and when they were asked whether their federal taxes were too high, 78 per cent said yes.

There is strong evidence that the middle American thinks he has certain material things coming to him, and the cry of the Los Angeles plumber—"Why, I can't even afford a color TV set!"—sticks in the mind like a line from an expert satirist. The middle American generally is not that extreme, but he clearly has a gnawing feeling that he is not getting what he deserves. The figures on his pay check tell him he is pretty well off, his training tells him that he deserves to be because he works hard, and the advertisements on television tell him that everybody else is.

Yet the truth is that many middle Americans are not affluent at all. The federal government estimates that a family of four needs $10,100 a year to maintain a moderate standard of living, and at least $4,345 to stay above the poverty level. Yet the median family income of married people in the United States is $9,144, and 41 per cent of all white families fall into the gray $5,000 to $10,000 bracket. These families feel the bite of inflation more keenly than those above them, and they are improving their economic status more slowly.

In 1968, men in the better-paying occupations increased their incomes by a far greater percentage than those in poor paying jobs. The income of professionals went up 6.2 per cent, that of clerical workers 7.8 per cent, that of craftsmen and foremen 6.5 per cent, and that of laborers (excluding farmers and miners) only 1.2 per cent.

For many of these lower middle income Americans, money is something that must be carefully and constantly watched. They are jealous of their union membership, because it is the only security they have, and they are resistant to Negro demands which seem to threaten that equity. They are jealous of their homes, because they are the largest investment they have, and they are resistent to Negro demands which seem to threaten the value of that investment. They are proud to think that they are doing well, but they have to watch supermarket ads in the papers, then buy forty pounds of ground beef and freeze it, because it is a special. They have worked hard for years, but for many of their raises there has been an off-setting increase in the cost of everything. Many of them do not go to the theater or even the movies. They do not throw cocktail parties, and they do not take trips. They do not go to beauty parlors or restaurants. They watch TV, where they are told that they are not enjoying the good life like everybody else.

"The pressure of wanting material things I don't have is always there," says a department store salesman in Springfield, Massachusetts, and the pressure of wanting often seems greater than the pressure of not being able to afford.

Meanwhile, in the view of many of these middle Americans, the Negro is getting a better chance than they themselves enjoy. The people on welfare are getting something for nothing. The kids in college, where they never had a chance to go, are burning records, throwing deans out the window, and calling cops "pigs." The liberals are calling him a racist; the establishment progressives, in their ivory suburbs, are telling him to integrate his schools before they have to integrate theirs; and the rich are getting out of taxes.

Perhaps it is not so surprising that he feels sorry for himself.

Yet when he casts about for people to blame for this sorry state of affairs, the middle American comes up almost empty-handed. In the *Newsweek* poll, 50 per cent gave the government a fair rating in handling the problems they faced, and another 22 per cent rated it good. Almost two-thirds said their schools were doing a good job of educating their children, and 87 per cent rated the schools at least fair. The identifiable villains all have flaws and limitations. The Negroes are a minority whose demands are partly justified, and so are the young. The welfare chiselers and the criminals have no justification but they live some place else, and even the angriest of middle Americans can hold them accountable for only a few of society's ills.

He fares no better when he looks for saviors. Faced on every side by things he disapproves of and resentful that nobody seems to be paying attention to him, the middle American would seem to be the stuff on which despots feed, yet he shows little appetite for extreme solutions. Politically, he is "a registered Undecided," as Bill Cosby said on a recent television show. He wants solutions, and he will probably follow anybody who seems to have them, but for the moment he is skeptical of all politicians.

There is a school of thought that the current President is made to order for such middle Americans. "Nixon is tremendously reassuring to middle class Americans," says Robert Nisbet, a sociologist at the University of California at Riverside. "If you started out to design a human being who would be an answer for this kind of person in this kind of time, you couldn't design a better one than Nixon. His kind of corny, square, ketchup-on-cottage-cheese image is very reassuring to these people."

But the *Newsweek* poll revealed more tolerance than enthusiasm for the President. Asked to rate his performance, nearly half graded it favorably, while another 31 per cent rated it fair, and only 15 per cent rated it poorly. But there was little zeal in the spoken comments about the President who calls the middle Americans "my people." "He's doing the best he can with the ability he has," said a housewife in Jacksonville, Florida, "which I don't think is too much."

There is nobody on the immediate horizon who looks any better. Only 12 per cent of the middle Americans thought the country would be better off with George Wallace as President, and only 10 per cent thought it would be in better shape under Hubert Humphrey.

One of the clearest indications of the *Newsweek* poll was that the middle Americans are products of the age of big government and, for all their griping, they wouldn't have it any other way. They may vote, eight to two, that federal taxes are too high. But when they were then asked what the government should do if an unexpected bonus showed up, only 34 per cent said they favored a tax cut, while another 16 per cent favored reducing the national debt, and 48 per cent said that the money should be used to improve conditions in the country. The ways in which they wanted government money to be spent also suggested that they wanted no slackening of efforts to help them or the under-privileged: they favored job training, Medicare, slum housing, programs to fight pollution, and crime control.

For the most part, for all the normal readiness to criticize "the politicians," most middle Americans seemed to feel that the government was doing the best it could. "It's not really the government's fault," said a Christmas-tree-bulb maker in Dorchester, Massachusetts. "The government can't solve everyone's problems."

"Many middle Americans even doubt their own ability to say how things ought to go in this complex society. A bare half of the *Newsweek* sample felt that they should have any say in the country's defense and foreign policies. "We are not well-informed enough to give solutions," said an accountant in Chicago.

There is scant encouragement in this resignation about the government's problem-solving capacity when it is set next to the middle American's view of his society. In the simplest terms, the middle American thinks his country is going downhill, and he sees very little that anybody can do about it. In the *Newsweek* poll, 46 per cent said that the country had changed for the worse in the past ten years, and only 36 per cent said that it had changed for the better. Seventy per cent believed that people are less religious than they were five years ago; 77 per cent said that the country's morality had changed for the worse; 86 per cent said that the emphasis on sex and nudity was undermining the country's morals at least some, and 62 per cent said that it was undermining morality a great deal. A salesman in Dallas summed up the majority feeling neatly: "Morality has gone to the devil," he said, "but living conditions have improved."

When he looks ahead, the middle American foresees still more prosperity and still more deterioration in the quality of life. Almost two-thirds of the *Newsweek* sample believed that in five years they would be at least as well off, or better off. But 58 per cent also believed that the country would change for the worse in spite of good times.

That is the sobering condition of the middle American today: the traditional backbone of the country finds little confidence in his country's future. Contemplating his society, he sees many of the same ills which the young, the black, and the intellectuals see, but unlike them, he has no doctrine for doing better, for reaching the promised land. He is no longer sure just where it is, and his faith in the old doctrines has been shaken. The hippies may proclaim their own new-found way of life, and the Negroes may declare that "Black is Beautiful." The middle American feels he is losing the only way of life he ever aimed for, and neither black nor white seems very beautiful any longer.

3

STANDARDS AND
SHIFTING SANDS

No people has ever been so hungry for change as the Americans. The country was founded and settled by people looking for a new way of life, and in their dash across the continent they altered everything to suit their fancy. They have reordered a good bit of one of the earth's biggest land masses, despoiled much of it, and plowed under the buildings of their new cities so fast that after two hundred years there are only a few that look old and established. They have invented the bulldozer and virtually turned it into a national emblem, and they change their surroundings so often that Richard Goodwin has observed that they have become nomadic even when staying in the same place. They outgrow houses and jobs the way children outgrow clothes, and one-fifth of them move every year. They want everything new, from laundry soaps to theories of psychiatry, and they have made energy and impatience their national characteristics. Yet, with all this evidence of their fickleness, they have persisted in thinking of themselves as slightly old-fashioned, with a fondness for old-fashioned girls and old-fashioned ways, and they have shown a split personality toward their own heritage.

"It is no mark of instability in us that Ford and Thoreau should both occupy places in our pantheon," Clifton Fadiman wrote confidently fifteen years ago. "We turn from one to the other, not because we are blind to the contradictions but because we are rich enough and varied enough in ourselves to be able to entertain that contradiction without schizophrenia." In this American pantheon, Thoreau stood for simplicity and permanence, Ford for complexity and change, and there was room for both.

But when the two came in conflict, it was usually Ford who won out. In that spirit, Americans have romanticized their small towns, and left them. They have looked for new frontiers, and resolutely tamed the ones they had. They have sung of the one girl meant just for them, and traded her in more often than any other people in the world. They have carried on about their love of the great outdoors, and moved into or near the big cities. They have preached the value of an honest day's work, and struck for the shortest hours possible. They have told their children about the good old days, and drive off in a new car to buy any product which claims that it has changed.

It may be that Americans loved change so much because it made them feel masterful. They could build a skyscraper and, if they didn't like it, tear it down and put up a new one. They could find a stream and, if they didn't like where it went, send it some place else. They could make a lake where one never was, and use it to turn a desert into farmland or a city. If they needed a city to make movies or take vacations in, they could build one. If the cities they built were too far apart, they could make fast airplanes that would bring them closer together. If they worked in a city and wanted to live in a small town, they could build superhighways that would connect them. And if they decided they wanted something new, they could overnight create an entire industry to make it. When the Indians traveled across America, they eradicated every sign that they had been there in order to leave nature undisturbed. When the white man moved across America, he did everything he could to rearrange nature to his own designs. Eric Hoffer, the philosopher of the masses, has said that it would be a wonderful thing if man could build a cabin on the highest peak of the highest Alp, so that all the world could see that he was in charge everywhere.

Whether something has happened to the process of change, or whether the Americans' split personality has simply caught up with them, most Americans no longer feel that they are in charge of change. The slave has become the master, and the former master is bewildered. Today, the change he once thought was limited to material things has spread to the area of morals, values, customs, religion, sex, patriotism, work, marriage, and everything else he felt old-fashioned about. For the first time, he finds he does not like change, and there seems to be nothing he can do about it.

It is easy to catalogue the specific changes that the middle American does not like. He was brought up to respect hard work; now millions are being given money for doing nothing, and affluent youngsters are announcing that work is nonsense. He was taught to behave well; now thousands of rebels shout filthy insults even at policemen. He always favored simple clothes; the new styles are garish and blatantly sexy. He always held to a strict code of public morality; now he can hardly walk down the street without seeing nudity and sex advertised. He was taught that children obeyed their parents; now they don't obey anybody. He was taught that drugs were used only by the debased; marijuana and much stronger drugs are now available almost everywhere. He thought the church was supposed to be a sanctuary of righteousness; now priests and ministers take to the streets to demonstrate for causes he doesn't believe in.

He thought that the flag was sacred and patriotism was a virtue; today, the flag is dragged and burned, millions protest against a war, and the term "super patriot" is one of scorn. He thought that Negroes were beneath him, whether they deserved to be or not; now he thinks they are getting favors denied to him. He believed in equal opportunity for all; now he hears black leaders asking for reparations for sins he doesn't believe he committed. He thought that owning your own car and house and minding your own business was a worthy goal; now he has reached it, and he finds himself ridiculed by young people and intellectuals. And he thought that the average man was the backbone of the country; now he feels himself scorned by many of the prominent and ignored by the rest.

Other changes are destroying his physical world. He always respected technology, and now it is befouling his air and his lakes. He expected technological systems to work, and they break down. He thought the country was enormous, and it suddenly seems to be jammed full of people. He thought that Americans could handle anything, and now mayors of great cities call them ungovernable and the country is lost in a war it can't seem to end. He thought Americans improved everything, and now they seem to be making things uglier.

It is bad enough that these changes have come about. But because they have come about, and because most of the people he knows didn't want them, the middle American is forced to conclude that neither he nor anybody else can control change any longer. It does not seem to be in the hands of people, even other people, but to have a life of its own. Things have turned upside down without anybody knowing how or having a method to set them to rights again.

In the opinion of many observers, this feeling of powerlessness in the face of change is the most insidious emotion at work in middle America today.

"You don't have cause and effect any more, all you have is probability," Saul Alinsky says. "Things no longer fit into neat slots of black and white. There is too much gray. The theory of relativity has created a political bomb more devastating than any nuclear bomb. It has knocked over our old set of values. All those fixed points that the middle class was weaned on—'If we bring up our children this way, then they will turn out this way'—they no longer apply. When a change like this starts to affect a group of a society, you either bend with it or stay where you are and get fractured. That's what's happening to the middle class. They're getting fractured."

"The average middle class guy feels," Dr. Jarl Dryud says, "that he's working too hard, getting too little pay, and getting hell from everybody, including his kids. He doesn't understand why and he's getting fed up. He's making more money than he ever has before, he has more creature comforts, yet he's still basically unhappy. He has less control over his government and his individual life than ever before. The natural reaction for anyone who continually gets knocked down is 'What the hell.' He stops trying. He stops working hard. He turns off. He looks for constant escapes and fantasies."

The feeling of powerlessness is not unique to middle America. In varying degrees it is shared by almost all Americans, and Richard Goodwin has described its effect on the individual citizen who has grown up thinking that he has some say over his own daily life:

"It would be hard to overstate the extent to which the malaise of powerlessness has eaten its way into our society, evoking an aimless unease, frustration, and fury. . . . The air around him is poisoned, parkland disappears under relentless bulldozers, traffic stalls and jams, airplanes cannot land, and even his own streets are unsafe and, increasingly, streaked with terror. Yet he cannot remember having decided that these things should happen, or even having wished them. He has no sense that there is anything he can do to arrest the tide. He does not know whom to blame. Somehow the crucial aspects of his environment seem in the grip of forces that are too huge and impersonal to attack. You cannot vote them out of office or shout them down. . . ."

If the middle American is not alone in his feeling of powerlessness, however, he probably feels it more acutely than any other group in society. The poor expect to be powerless, and their concern with getting the basic necessities is even stronger than their concern with their environment. The wealthy may have no more control over events, but they have the power of flight. They can escape to the more affluent suburbs, where they can limit change by limiting growth. The middle American has an income that should entitle him to a pleasant life, yet he often does not get it, and he lacks the freedom to move someplace else.

"These are the people who perhaps earn more than they have ever earned in the past but who are not secure, who bear the major brunt of rising taxes and carry the heaviest burden of inflation," Joseph Duffey, the National Chairman of the ADA, has said. "The safety of their neighborhoods is most in jeopardy because of inadequate law enforcement. Their children go to crowded schools. They must swim in polluted rivers and bays and depend upon crowded public transportation. They often have to travel great distances for decent recreation. . . . These people have legitimate reason to protest what is going on in American society, and yet they have been neglected by liberal movements and by both political parties. For in a sense, liberalism has become an activity of the affluent for whom the concerns of these people, like the concerns of the very poor, emerge primarily in abstract terms and categories."

The relentless deterioration of his physical world is a source of daily aggravation to the middle American, and concern for the environment is no longer the special province of conservationists. "Of the people I talked to," Karl Fleming wrote after five weeks in middle America, "the most frustrated and angry were those trapped in spirit-numbing jobs and neighborhoods besieged by pollution, noise, traffic, decay and crime. The happiest were those whose jobs gave them relief from tedium, and a chance to live near open fields and green trees, sunlight, creeks and country roads." "You can go thirty miles into the country and get away from it," truck driver Fred Huff said, contemplating the steel mills and oil refineries of Hammond, Indiana. "But then it costs too much to commute."

If the decay of his physical world were the only sign of the middle American's impotence, he would have plenty of reason for anger and frustration. It is not the only sign, and it may not even be the most important. The middle American also sees all his old standards of behavior crumbling, and he feels powerless to do anything about that, either. His impotence in the face of decaying morals and values is even greater and lonelier than his impotence against physical decay, because while no one welcomes physical pollution, the changing standards of behavior seem to be welcomed and even espoused by many of the rich, the liberals, and sometimes even his own children. The changes in accepted standards are not the work of faceless forces but of people, and the middle American sometimes feels that he is the only one objecting. Most unsettling of all, those promoting the new standards are saying that the old-fashioned middle American has been barking up the wrong tree, and the suspicion has clearly occurred to the middle American himself. He has always followed the rules, but they have not brought him where he wanted to be, and now they are being changed. It is as though he had scrimped for years to buy a powerful new car, and then, when he got it home, the engine fell out in his driveway.

"The radicals are a group of people whose values are totally opposite the ones that the middle group thinks it has embraced since childhood," says Dr. Anthony Downs, an urban economist in Chicago. "When these radical thoughts are magnified through television, it becomes a terribly powerful, direct attack on them. The guy sits there looking at all this on the tube and he says, 'Well, if it's not true that work and family and the flag are good ideas, then my whole life has been a joke.' Who can face that without getting restive and angry?"

"When the hippies go to Woodstock, they are building a

new community of their own," says Paul Jacobs. "The worker's community is disintegrating. He doesn't know where to find a new one. So he keeps harking back to the old days and the old values. But it is not possible to go back. And there is no new community to replace the old. The workers resent the new community that others have found. They don't have one of their own."

"Middle class values that we held so dear—and were pretty much a myth—are being shot to hell," says George Culberson, deputy director of the Community Relations Service in Washington. "Everything's being attacked—what you believed in, what you learned in school, in church, from your parents. So the middle class is sort of losing heart. We were so sure we were on the right track. Things were more simple two or three years ago when everyone thought when we got the black-white problem solved we'd come out all right. Now it's obvious, even if we solve it, so what? The lower middle class whites are more threatened by change in status than anyone else. They had an eye on where they were going and suddenly it's all shifting sands."

The middle Americans registered their distaste for recent changes in a series of questions in the *Newsweek* poll. On the materialistic level, they felt, generally, that things were going well. When they were asked whether things were better or worse for people like themselves than they were five years ago, 36 per cent said better, 37 per cent said about the same, and 25 per cent said worse. When they were asked to rate their own prospects for the immediate future, 34 per cent expected things to get better, 30 per cent expected them to stay about the same, and 28 per cent expected things to get worse. But when they were asked to rate their country's prospects for the future, 58 per cent saw a considerable amount or a fair amount of danger that the country would change for the worse (26 per cent said there was considerable danger, 32 per cent said there was a fair amount of danger), 18 per cent said there was little danger, and 14 per cent said there was hardly any danger at all.

Q. HOW MUCH DANGER DO YOU THINK THERE IS THAT IN
THE YEARS AHEAD THIS COUNTRY MIGHT BE CHANGED
FOR THE WORSE—CONSIDERABLE DANGER, A FAIR
AMOUNT, LITTLE, OR HARDLY ANY AT ALL?

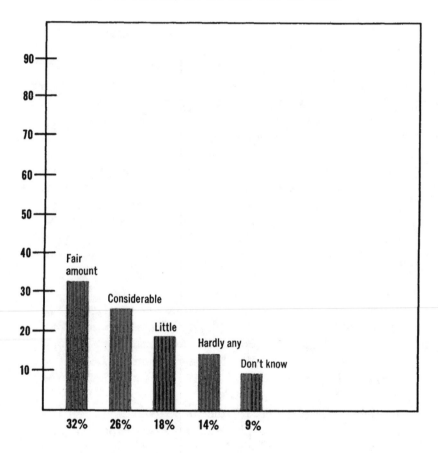

Similarly, when they were asked whether the country had changed for the better or the worse in the ten years past, a plurality of 46 per cent said it had changed for the worse, 36 per cent said it had changed for the better, and 13 per cent saw no difference.

When they specifically considered the nation's moral and religious feelings, the pessimism grew sharper. Seventy-seven per cent thought that standards of morality had changed for the worse, and only 10 per cent thought they had changed for the better. Eighty-six per cent said that nudity and sexual permissiveness were weakening the country's moral fiber, and 70 per cent said that people are less religious than they were five years ago. In a nation-wide Gallup poll in May 1969, 74 per cent of the sampling said they would find pictures of nudes in magazines objectionable, 77 per cent said they would object to topless nightclub waitresses, and 82 per cent said they would be offended by seeing actors and actresses in the nude in Broadway plays.

The middle Americans are in the majority in the nation, and with eight out of ten in agreement, they should be able to stand up and call a halt to the moral laxity they think is dragging the country down. Yet the middle Americans have lost confidence in each other, too. In the *Newsweek* poll, they were asked how many people really care what happens to strangers. The largest number, 33 per cent, said "hardly anybody," and the smallest number, 16 per cent, said "most." About 39 per cent said most or about half, while 59 per cent said some or hardly anybody.

They did not feel much more confident about their own neighbors. When they were asked whether they thought people in their neighborhood would come to their aid if they were being robbed or attacked, 30 per cent said that help was very likely, 30 per cent said help was fairly likely, and 38 per cent said help was not too likely or not likely at all.

The middle Americans also have little faith in their sources of information. Their hostility toward the news media has often been noted, but in the *Newsweek* poll the middle

Q. TO WHAT EXTENT DO YOU THINK THE MORALS OF THIS
    COUNTRY ARE BEING UNDERMINED BY THE CURRENT
    EMPHASIS ON SEX AND NUDITY IN THE MOVIES, THEA-
    TERS, BOOKS, AND MAGAZINES—A GREAT DEAL, SOME,
    A LITTLE, OR NOT AT ALL?

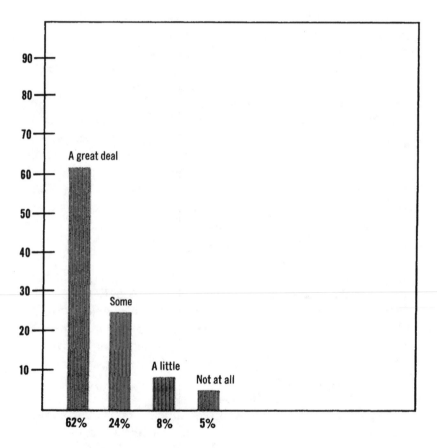

Q.   DO YOU THINK MOST PEOPLE TODAY ARE MORE RELI-
     GIOUS OR LESS RELIGIOUS THAN THEY WERE FIVE YEARS
     AGO?

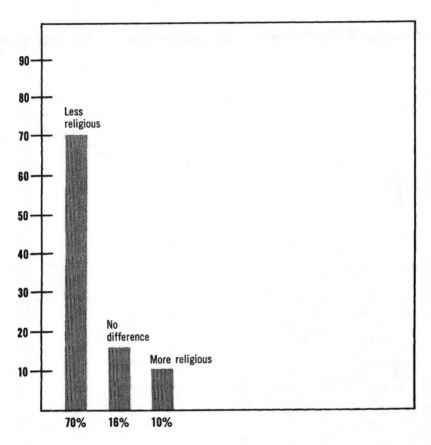

Q. HOW MANY PEOPLE TODAY DO YOU THINK REALLY CARE
WHAT HAPPENS TO PEOPLE THEY DON'T KNOW PERSON-
ALLY—DO MOST PEOPLE CARE, ABOUT HALF, SOME, OR
HARDLY ANYBODY?

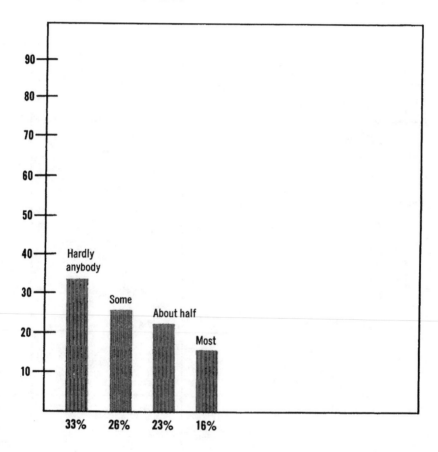

33% 26% 23% 16%

Americans showed the same suspiciousness toward the government itself. When they were asked whether they trusted the news media to tell them the truth about what is going on in the world today, only 14 per cent trusted the media a great deal, 55 per cent trusted them some, and 29 per cent trusted them little or not at all. When they were asked how much they trusted the government to tell them the truth, the results were almost exactly the same: only 13 per cent trusted it a great deal, while 51 per cent trusted it some, and 32 per cent trusted it little or not at all.

Taken together, these answers reveal a sizeable degree of alienation from American society. They think the country has lost its way morally and religiously, they do not trust their prime sources of information, and they do not trust each other.

Given a society in which so many unreliable forces are at work, the middle Americans might be expected to be even more pessimistic and alienated than they are. But the middle American tends to exempt himself and his immediate family from his harsh judgments. "We keep talking about permissiveness in training kids," says a labor official in Los Angeles, "but we forget that these are our kids."

The *Newsweek* poll also suggested that the middle Americans may not be quite as exercised about morality and religion as they profess to be. Although a consistent 70 per cent to 80 per cent expressed dismay at the country's moral condition, the middle Americans put moral and religious problems far down on their list of the major problems facing the country. In order of frequency of mention, they put Vietnam first, civil rights and race second, the high cost of living third, taxes fourth, poverty and slums fifth, youth protests sixth, crime and delinquency seventh, national unrest eighth, and moral and religious problems ninth. In their own communities, they showed even less concern: the problems they listed were, in order, high taxes, inflation, civil rights and race, education, transportation, housing, youth problems and delinquency, crime—and in 21st place, after such problems as sanitation and recreation, morality and religion. In other words, two out of three middle Americans think the country's morals are being undermined a great deal by sex and nudity, but only one in thirty considers that one of the country's three most important problems, and fewer than one in fifty considers it a major problem in his own community.

Without detailed studies, there is no way to reconcile this contradiction, but there are several possible explanations. One is that the middle American is engaging in a bit of tongue-clucking and cares about the new morality somewhat less than he claims. Another is that he sees moral permissiveness as the work of a radical few, and reserves his special condemnation for them. A third is that he simply does not yet think of morality in terms of "national problems" because he sees little or no role for the government in dealing with it. And a fourth is that, with so many practical troubles on his mind, the problem of morality simply gets squeezed far down on his list.

The new moral permissiveness may or may not have become a personal problem to the middle American, but the shifting standards of behavior has become a very personal one. Even within his own sphere of influence, the middle American finds values changing. In many middle income families, the wife today has a job to supplement the husband's income. In the past twenty years, the number of white collar working women has doubled, from eight to sixteen million. These working wives bring a touch of affluence, but it is often affluence with a price. The notion of women working clashes with the middle American's concept of the woman's role and, writes Irving Levine of the American Jewish Committee, "contributes to a sense of disorientation and alienation."

Moreover, the women of the working class are sometimes changing their own life styles. They often want a livelier social life and more social participation from their husbands. The working class man, often, doesn't really want to partici-

pate: He looks on his home as a refuge from the pressures of
the world, and he has no desire to become a social butterfly.
Sociologists say that the working class man typically sets
great store by silence and emotional control, which he considers manly virtues. He thus feels that even at home, he is
being asked to act in ways which are not natural to him.

Meanwhile, the social world of the man has been changing, too. In the old days, the labor union, the political club,
and the church functioned as buffers between the working
man and the outside world. Today, these organizations have
generally become large and anonymous or, in the case of the
political club, have almost vanished.

"I haven't given the church a penny in two years," says
Ray Walczak, the gig grinder in Milwaukee. "They're supposed to teach kids to love thy neighbor, not all this racial
stuff. I despise them now. If they want to bury me in the
Catholic church, fine. If not, tough."

"I used to go to church and the preacher would talk about
God, Jesus, and the Bible," said a man in Minneapolis.
"Now he tells me why I shouldn't buy grapes." When the
Archdiocese of Detroit pledged to give one million dollars
in aid to the blacks and the poor, many white Catholics sim-
ply withheld their contributions to the Church.

Many sociologists believe that this disruption of traditional guideposts is most acute at the lower end of the middle
class spectrum, and the *Newsweek* poll bore them out. On a
number of questions, the wealthier, the better educated, and
the white collar workers showed notably less alienation from
their society than their poorer, less well educated, blue collar
counterparts.

On the basic question of the country's ability to solve its
problems, confidence decreased as income, education, and
occupation level decreased. In the national sample, of those
earning more than $15,000, 42 per cent were more confident
and 34 per cent were less confident, while those earning less
than $5,000 voted the opposite: 45 per cent less confident,
32 per cent more confident. In middle America, those under

30 were more confident by a 45 per cent to 36 per cent margin, while those over 55 were less confident by 49 per cent to 30 per cent. Similarly, 47 per cent of the white collar workers and only 37 per cent of the blue collar workers were more confident, and the split was even more pronounced in the $5,000 to $10,000 bracket. But education level produced the biggest split of all. Exactly half of those with some college education felt more confident, and only 31 per cent were less confident. But among those whose education ended at grade school, only 25 per cent were more confident—and 52 per cent were less confident.

The wealthy, the college educated, and those in white collar jobs were also more inclined to think that at least some people care what happens to strangers, while the poor, the under educated, and the blue collar workers were more inclined to say that hardly anybody cares. The members of the first group were more inclined to say that the country had changed for the better in the past ten years, they were more inclined to trust the government and the news media, and they were less inclined to think that nudity and sex were seriously undermining the nation's morals.

Even greater differences occurred on a question about the need for experimentation in solving the nation's problems. "Some people say that we need to experiment with new ways of dealing with the nation's problems," the questionnaire said. "Others say that there has been too much experimentation already. Which side do you agree with more?" Fifty-eight per cent of the wealthy on the national sample favored experimentation, but only 31 per cent of the poor. Fifty-eight per cent of the young favored experimentation, and only 37 per cent of the old. Fifty-eight per cent of the white collar workers favored experimentation, and only 46 per cent of the blue collar workers. And 63 per cent of those with some college education favored experimenting, compared to only 30 per cent of those who never went past grade school.

The greatest differences of all came on a question con-

Standards and Shifting Sands

Q. COMPARED WITH FIVE YEARS AGO, DO YOU FEEL MORE CONFIDENT OR LESS CONFIDENT ABOUT THE ABILITY OF THIS COUNTRY TO SOLVE ITS PROBLEMS?

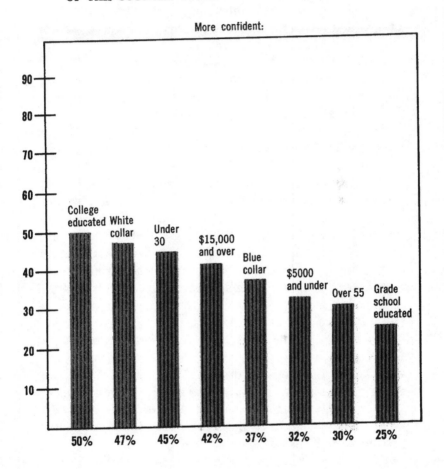

62 /

THE TROUBLED AMERICAN

cerning young people. In the middle America sample generally, 58 per cent said their opinion of young people today was favorable. Of those with some college education, 66 per cent had a favorable opinion and only 15 per cent were unfavorable, while those who had not gone past grade school were evenly split—34 per cent favorable, 33 per cent unfavorable. Of the white collar workers earning $5,000 to $10,000 a year, 63 per cent were favorable, while only 53 per cent of their blue collar counterparts were favorable. Income level was the most important factor of all. Almost three-fourths of those earning more than $15,000 looked on the young favorably, compared to 58 per cent of the middle Americans and only 42 per cent of the poor.

On other questions about recent changes in American society there was little disagreement. All the middle Americans agreed by a wide margin that the country's morals had changed for the worse. All agreed that people were less religious than they used to be, and the young were notably more inclined to say so than their elders. All showed some skepticism about the amount of help they could expect from their neighbors if they were attacked. Even where differences existed, they were often only a matter of degree. In all categories within middle America, large numbers of people registered their dislike of recent changes in their society and their fear of the future, and at the lower end of the middle American spectrum, these dislikes and fears were acute.

In this unsettled state, the middle American bitterly resents those who seem to be causing the troubling changes around him. He is not able to identify many such villains, but those he finds are coming in for a good deal of animosity and even hatred. Saul Alinsky has said that, in his bewildered state, the middle American is developing a capacity for hating "blindly, not knowing what, just turning on the hate at anything or anyone that doesn't subscribe to his particular view of the world."

The threat of change may even be dividing America in subtle ways that have barely been recognized. "I don't iden-

Q. IS YOUR OPINION OF MOST YOUNG PEOPLE TODAY FAVORABLE OR UNFAVORABLE?

Favorable:

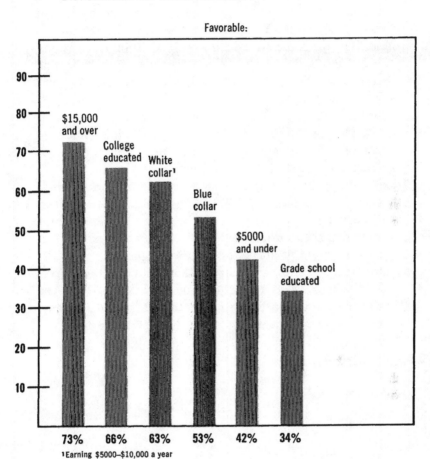

73% 66% 63% 53% 42% 34%

[1] Earning $5000–$10,000 a year

tify people as conservative or liberal any more," says Reverend Dorel Londagin of the Christ Presbyterian Church in San Leandro, California. "I call them change or no-change people. And most people around here are scared and uptight. They think the American way of life is pretty precious, and that if we don't solidify and stabilize it, we'll lose it. Therefore we must not question any part of life. We must maintain the status quo."

Declaring a moratorium on change is probably an impossibility in contemporary America, but the middle American can at least declare emotional war on those who seem to be creating unwanted change, and that is just what he often does. "We've had a series of problems since World War II that just won't let up," Dr. Abraham Kaplan of the University of Michigan says, "and people want more than anything to think that these problems do not exist. So they direct their anger not at the problems but at the people who won't let them forget the problems. They look around and say, 'We've entered paradise, and it looks like the place we just left. And if this is paradise, why am I so miserable? Maybe it's because all these people are running around telling me it's bad.' "

4

THE TROUBLEMAKERS

One of the memorable news photographs of 1964 showed two defendants sitting in a Mississippi courtroom where they were being charged with conspiracy to deprive three civil rights workers of their rights by murdering them. One man was smiling broadly. The other was slumped casually, a booted foot on one knee, one hand holding a bag of Red Man chewing tobacco, the other hand dipping into it, a wad of tobacco bulging out his cheek, and his mouth open in laughter. Behind them, spectators in the courtroom were grinning and looking at each other knowingly. Without benefit of a caption, the defendants might have been taken for two men relishing a stag movie in the company of friends.

Outside an auto body shop in San Leandro, California, in 1969, Frank Reis and David Pedroza, partners in a house repair business, and David Linton, the shop owner, stood kicking their toes in the gravel and waiting for a truck to be fixed.

"Look at those riots," David Pedroza said. "What the fuck do you think would happen to us if we went over there and started a riot?"

"They'd kill us," Frank Reis said.

"Fucking right they would," Pedroza said.

"Paint your face black and you can get a new Cadillac and the county will come in and feed your family," Reis said. "What do they call it? Prejudice or something? That's all they've got to holler and they've got it made. Let a fucking patrolman stop me and I've got to pay."

"What do you think would happen to us if we went around calling police 'pigs'?" David Linton demanded. "And let me be starving and steal a loaf of bread and they'd throw my ass in jail. There's nobody behind us hollering 'prejudice.' "

"There's only one way to solve this, and that's gonna be with a revolution," Pedroza said. "I'm for fighting it out between us."

"I'd go for that," Reis said. "Just give me a machine gun."

"What do you call dragging the American flag on the ground and burning draft cards and all that crap?" Reis demanded.

"Treason," Pedroza said.

"We should have a Hitler here to get rid of the troublemakers," Reis said, "the way they did with the Jews in Germany."

Many things have changed in the mind of the middle American during the 1960's, but none of the changes has been as radical as the shift in his outlook toward himself, on the one hand, and those he considers troublemakers, on the other. In the early sixties, when civil rights marches and sit-ins in the South were being met with police dogs and bombings, many whites sympathized with the Negro, and those who didn't felt cocky about their ability to handle the situation. From different vantage points, almost everybody saw the Negro as an underdog. By the end of the decade, a near majority of middle Americans had come to look on the Negro as a man who was getting preferential treatment at their expense. The underdog had become the favorite, and they, who had looked down with either sympathy or scorn, were now looking up. They did not like the feeling.

It is almost impossible to make this view square with any of the facts. The American Negro earns, on the average, 60 per cent as much as the white American. His chances of being poor are four times as good: 34.5 per cent of all non-white families fall in the poverty class, as opposed to 8 per cent of all whites. The Negro stands half as good a chance of going to college. He has three times as good a chance of dying in childhood, and at 25 his life expectancy is more than five years shorter than a white man's. Theoretically, he stands an equal chance of getting unemployment compensation; whether his chances are better or poorer in practice is impossible to say. His chances of getting into a skilled union are much worse, and sometimes non-existent: the Negro's membership in the plumbers and sheet metal workers union, the barbers union, and the electrical workers union is less than 1 per cent, while his membership in the building trades laborers union is 30 per cent. His chances of living in sub-standard housing are almost four times as great as a white man's, and he pays proportionately more for the housing he gets. In large cities, he stands a greater chance of living in a poor neighborhood: two-thirds of all non-whites in poverty areas are not poor themselves. His chances of escaping to the suburbs are much worse.

Yet most middle Americans are convinced, or claim to be, that the Negro has a better chance than they do in at least one or two basic areas. Most middle Americans think the Negro could have helped himself and didn't. After all these years and all the talk of discrimination, many and perhaps most middle Americans now feel discriminated against.

The middle American also says that people on welfare live better than he does, and he is convinced they could earn their own way if they wanted to. He thinks young demonstrators and black militants are getting away with things that would land him in jail. He thinks criminals are mollycoddled by the law. Aiding and abetting these blatant troublemakers, he frequently sees a phalanx of appeasers, cheats, connivers, and hypocrites: the rich, the liberals, the politicians, the government in general, the courts, the press, the professors, and others he can't even make out. Taken together, these people form a shadowy enemy, linked vaguely and only by their ability to do him out of what is rightfully his.

But he doesn't know what to do about it. He sometimes talks about standing up and letting them have it, and instead just keeps on talking. He sometimes talks about buying guns, but he seldom does it. He often says we should get rid of the troublemakers, but he doesn't say how.

And, basically, he doesn't know whom to blame for this mess. The actual troublemakers are a minority, the coalition behind them is too shadowy to get at, and most of the villains of populism past have vanished. In earlier days, these enemies of the common people were big business, Catholics, big city people, foreigners, and Communists. But too many middle Americans now get a good livelihood from big business, their most idoilzed recent President was a Catholic, 80 per cent of them are big city people themselves, one-fifth of them are foreigners or the children of foreigners and are as mad as the rest, while the self-proclaimed spokesman for the forgotten man, once one of the most fervid anti-Communists in the land, is now in the White House speaking softly and calling for peaceful competition with the Reds.

Yet the middle American is left with his resentments, and justified or not, they are real. Some of the time, he may be simply letting off steam, but he has a big head of steam to let off. "We're in a race against time," says Representative Allard Lowenstein, whose Long Island constituency is mainly composed of middle Americans. "They look for scapegoats and find them, and it's not always the Negro. If anyone's to be excluded, they want it to be someone other than themselves."

So the new target of middle America's animosity is the loose coalition it can only define as "the troublemakers": the Negroes, the people on welfare, some of the young, the criminals, the press, the liberals and their allies. They have little in common, and the middle Americans cannot really persuade himself that they are linked in some sort of conspiracy. They do not make first-rate villains, but they are all he has.

The most startling result of the *Newsweek* poll was the unmistakable evidence that most middle Americans feel that the Negro is now getting more than his fair share, at least in some areas. In a 1963 *Newsweek* poll, almost two-thirds of all whites felt that Negro job opportunities and education were worse than their own, and almost three-fourths believed that Negro housing was poorer. Only four years ago, a *Newsweek* poll showed that two out of three white Americans believed that Negro was wrongly discriminated against. Two-thirds felt that Negro housing was poorer, 46 per cent sympathized with current Negro protests, 70 per cent expected to be living in integrated housing in five years time, and large majorities approved of federal legislation to insure equal voting rights (91 per cent), the right to a fair jury trial (87 per cent), and integrated education (72 per cent).

The contrast between these findings and those of 1969 is dramatic. Of the middle Americans surveyed in 1969, 44 per cent said that Negroes now had a *better* chance than they did of getting a well-paying job, 41 per cent felt that Negroes had a better chance for a good education, 35 per cent felt that Negroes had a better chance for good housing at a reasonable price, and 65 per cent felt that Negroes had a better chance for financial help from the government when they were out of work. Equally startling, only one in five felt the black man's chance for a job were actually worse, only one in six thought his chances for a good education were worse, fewer than one in three thought his chances for housing were worse, and only one in twenty-five thought his chances for unemployment help were worse.

The resentment suggested by those answers came out even more forcefully on other questions. Of the middle Americans surveyed, 85 per cent felt that black militants had been dealt with too leniently, 55 per cent felt the black man could have done something about his own employment, and 73

Q. IN YOUR OPINION, DO NEGROES TODAY HAVE A BETTER
CHANCE OR A WORSE CHANCE THAN PEOPLE LIKE YOUR-
SELF TO GET WELL-PAYING JOBS?

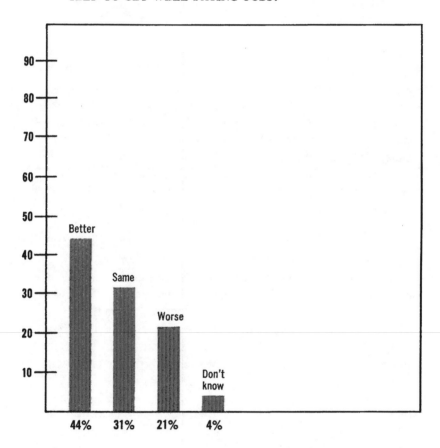

Q. IN YOUR OPINION, DO NEGROES TODAY HAVE A BETTER
CHANCE OR A WORSE CHANCE THAN PEOPLE LIKE YOUR-
SELF TO GET FINANCIAL HELP FROM THE GOVERNMENT
WHEN THEY'RE OUT OF WORK?

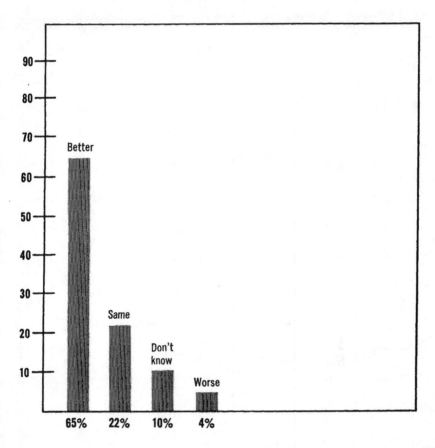

Q.   IN YOUR OPINION, HAVE BLACK MILITANTS BEEN DEALT
     WITH TOO SEVERELY OR TOO LENIENTLY?

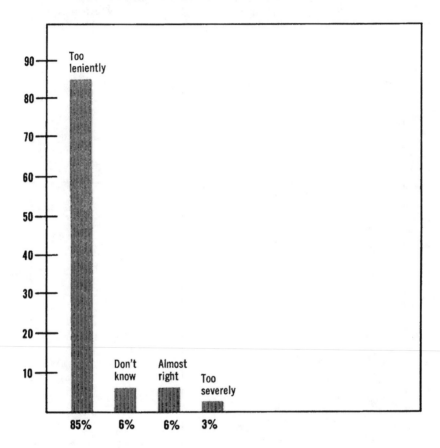

Q. DO YOU THINK THAT CONDITIONS THAT NEGROES HAVE HAD TO LIVE WITH IN THE SLUMS ARE SOMETHING THEY HAVE HAD TO PUT UP WITH, OR COULD THEY HAVE DONE SOMETHING ABOUT THOSE CONDITIONS THEMSELVES?

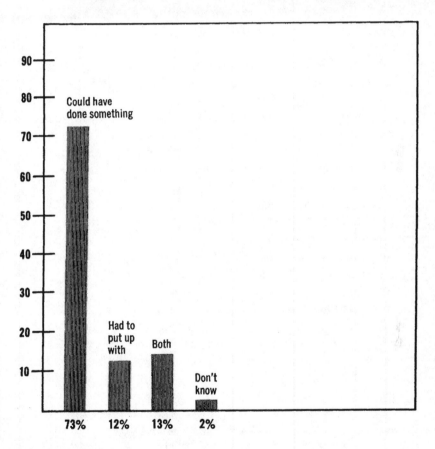

per cent felt the black man could have done something about his slum conditions.

Other polls have gotten similar results. In September 1969, a Louis Harris poll asked, "Do you feel that Negroes are discriminated against in the way they are treated as human beings or not?" Of the whites polled, 35 per cent said Negroes were discriminated against and 54 per cent said they weren't.

Statistical poll results sometimes show more apparent than real unanimity, and the *Newsweek* results were not quite as consistent as they appear. Of those who said the Negro had a better chance than they did of getting a good job, only 58 per cent *also* said the Negro's chances for good housing were better, while 18 per cent said they were worse. But even though the composition changed from category to category, the largest number of middle Americans saw favoritism at work in each of the four categories. In other words, most middle Americans do not believe that the Negro has it over them in all four categories, but most think he has it over them in at least one or two categories, and a substantial minority thinks the Negro has it over them in all four.

Similar variations, moreover, showed up among those who were most sympathetic to black demands. Of those who thought the Negro's chances for a good job and education were worse than their own, 85 per cent also said that at least some Negro demands were justified, as opposed to 70 per cent in middle America generally. But even among these relatively sympathetic middle Americans, more than half felt that the Negro could have done something to improve his own living conditions; about 70 per cent thought that half or more of the people getting welfare could earn their keep if they wanted to; and about 77 per cent felt that black militants had been dealt with too leniently.

There is also a strong strain of simple prejudice within middle America, and, fueled by the new feeling of being victimized, it is finding fresh expression. There is again open talk of genetic differences between the races, and it is heard not only in the South. "One has to consider the evidence that the Negro may be inherently inferior to the white and incapable of competing with him," says a professor at M.I.T. "Look at the ones who have succeeded. They're almost all light colored." In one poll of male, white, school children in the South after Martin Luther King's assassination, a shocking 73 per cent reported either indifference or pleasure. In comments to poll-takers and reporters, deep animosities sometimes bubbled to the surface. "I see it every day," said a Supreme Court clerk in the Bronx. "They are on relief. They don't want to work. They get up in the morning and decide, 'Who am I going to kill today?' " Many of the letters to *Newsweek* after its "Troubled American" issues were violent. "I would rather see my beautiful country of America destroyed by the atom bomb than polluted, infested, contaminated and diseased by the black cancer," wrote a man in Virginia.

Such hatred is not limited to the South; it pours from people in all parts of the country and in all walks of life. Sometimes it is an expression of fear ("We are really afraid, with the colored right in our back yard"). Sometimes it is the product of white supremacy ("We fascists are getting sick and tired of the colored who won't leave well enough alone and stay in their place"). But, sometimes, many sociologists believe, it is the product of ethnic animosity which is neither better nor worse than the animosity which the Irish had for the Italians and the Italians for the Poles.

"They feel betrayed in another way," Paul Jacobs says. "They had always considered themselves good Americans. Good Americans, that is, along the traditional ethnic model: they would curse niggers, hate Jews, and look down on all the non-white minorities. Now suddenly society says to them, 'You can't do this any more.' " Black demands, Jacobs believes, have helped to liberate feelings that were always there but were covert. "They've always been anti-Negro," he says, "but they've never been pressed to say it publicly before.

Part of the myth was that if we could get 'em to work together, we could get 'em to like each other. Well, whites and Negroes have worked together. But they still don't like each other."

White efforts to improve the Negro's lot have sometimes aggravated these animosities by ignoring a fundamental consideration: The white sponsors have failed to take a hard look at the price and the question of who is going to pay for the improvement, and the middle American often feels he is being forced to carry out other people's good deeds. John Roche has described the failing clearly: "A and B agree on something which is at C's and D's expense. For example, Lindsay and Bundy do something for the Negroes at the expense of the 72 per cent of the population of New York that is not Negro. When the lower middle class majority gets mad, they're called racists. But there is only the same animosity as between the Irish and the Italians. They look on the massive inroads of the Negroes and say, 'Look, we didn't make it that far that fast.' "

"Integration to John Lindsay," a Jackson Heights, New York, man wrote *Newsweek*, "is lunch with Ralph Bunche and a low-cost housing project around the corner from somebody else."

The argument that other ethnic groups gained acceptance more slowly than the Negro is patently untrue, if one starts the stopwatch at the time of their arrival in this country, but it is true that they made it largely without government aid. Moreover, there are still many poor whites, and they do not seem to middle America to be getting the same attention as the black man. "Twice as many whites as blacks in New York City are in poverty," Roche says, "yet all the great concentration of conversation is that poverty is uniquely black. This is resented by the whites, and by the Puerto Ricans, also. The ethnic groups, Irish and Jews, don't want to penalize the Negro, but they feel strongly that the rules they came up by should apply. To change the rules now is basically unfair. The middle class generally feels that their virtues are not appreciated—that's why the bumper stickers and flags. They have a feeling they aren't getting the recognition they deserve."

Of all the areas where black aspirations meet white resistance, none is more difficult than the area of jobs. Professor Richard Wade, an urban historian at the University of Chicago, notes that such competition between races has been increasing.

"Since 1945, most of the new jobs have come in the suburbs," he says. "The actual number of jobs in the city has been shrinking. The blacks who are trapped in the cities have no shot at all for those suburban jobs, so they become competitors for the jobs that do exist inside the cities. And these have been held by white workers." Many unions have built up apprenticeship programs which are not very subtly designed to keep newcomers from taking away their members' jobs: the programs, particularly in the building trades, are long, tedious, and pay poorly. "The only way whites could accept blacks," Professor Wade says, "is if somebody could *guarantee* that there would be enough jobs, and this is where the Nixon administration has failed—cutting back federal building programs, letting interest rates soar so high that home building slows down, this threatens jobs and aggravates the black-white controversy."

The working man's jealousy over his job and union membership may or may not be defensible, but it is a fact, and one which is probably not going to change. According to Robert Wood, the director of the Joint Center for Urban Studies, the working American is not concerned with his country, his community, or his neighborhood but with his job, his family, and his home. Wood was one of the first to address himself to the problems of the working white American when, as Under Secretary of Housing and Urban Development, he delivered the Bemis Lecture outside Boston three years ago. In it, he described the gulf between the white working man and the liberal coalition whom he called "the pro-urbanites."

"The working American," Wood said, "is the one who most typically refuses to open his neighborhood to minorities, denies their entrance into his unions, rejects the idea of minorities going to school with his children, and votes against the pro-urbanite's candidate for office. Yet, until and unless the working American joins the process of community building, the process cannot succeed. So the hard question comes: Has the pro-urbanite unconsciously alienated the working man from his community? Has he been given equal time as we respond to the vocal spokesmen of the minority groups? Have viable alternatives been available in elections? Or has he been lost in the shuffle of self-righteous efforts?"

Wood then noted that the working man's concerns were not with remote causes but with his immediate responsibilities of home and job. "To the pro-urbanite, these preoccupations may seem outdated, self-centered. But the typical citizen is made aware that he has only labor, not capital, as a source for the well-being of his family and children. He knows that whatever his legacy may be, it will not typically include stocks, securities, or real estate holdings to his children." He then quoted a letter from a union member to *The New York Times*:

"Some men leave their sons money, some large investments, some business connections, and some a profession. I have only one worthwhile thing to give: my trade. I hope to follow a centuries-old tradition and sponsor my son for an apprenticeship. For this simple father's wish it is said I discriminate against Negroes. Don't all of us discriminate? Which of us . . . will not choose a son over all others?

"I believe that an apprenticeship in my union is no more a public trust, to be shared by all, than a millionaire's money is a public trust. Why should the government, be it local, state, or federal, have any more right to decide how I dispose of my heritage than it does how the corner grocer disposes of his?"

"The hunger for job security," Wood commented, "does

not make the working man a hero—but neither does it stamp him as a bigot."

Most middle Americans, in fact, are not racists, at least in the old sense of the word, and they have a good deal of sympathy for black aspirations. In the *Newsweek* poll, almost seven out of ten middle Americans said that there was at least some justification for black demands, although it will take some time to meet them. The respondents in the poll were asked to pick one of five statements which best described their feelings about the demands being made by black leaders. A majority of 56 per cent checked the statement "Some of these demands are justified, but it will take some time to meet them." Another 12 per cent said that "Most of these demands are justified, but it will take some time to meet them." Nineteen per cent said that "Very few of these demands are justified, and they have pretty much been taken care of." Seven per cent said the demands were completely unjustified, and one per cent said they were completely justified.

In fact, there is good evidence that pure racism, instead of increasing, is actually on the decrease in middle America. A July 1969 Gallup poll showed a major shift in the number of people who would vote for a Negro for President, from 38 per cent of all adults in 1958 to 53 per cent of white adults in 1965 to 65 per cent of white adults in 1969. Other Gallup studies have indicated that opposition toward school integration is based primarily on fears of a deterioration in the quality of education: There is acceptance of Negroes in school provided there are not too many.

Even in the South in recent years, this attitude has replaced the traditional opposition to any form of integrated schooling. In a 1963 Gallup poll of white Southerners, 78 per cent said they would object to half-black, half-white schools, and 61 per cent would object to having even a few black students. By 1969, only 46 per cent said they would object to a racially balanced school, and only 21

Q.   WHICH ONE STATEMENT ON THIS CARD BEST DESCRIBES
     YOUR FEELINGS ABOUT THE DEMANDS BEING MADE BY
     NEGRO LEADERS THESE DAYS?

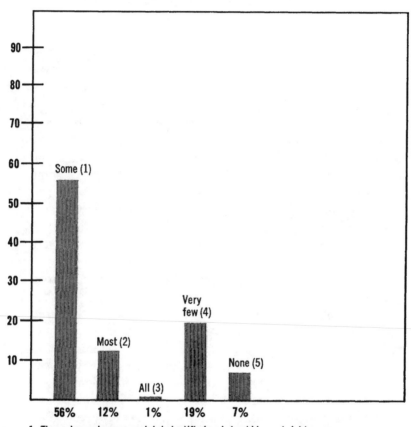

1. These demands are completely justified and should be met right away.
2. Most of these demands are justified, but it will take some time to meet them.
3. Some of these demands are justified, but it will take some time to meet them.
4. Very few of these demands are justified, and they have pretty much been taken care of.
5. These demands are competely unjustified and they should not be granted.

per cent would object to having any black students at all.

What seems to have happened in recent years is that resentment over black demands has built up even while pure racial antagonism has declined, and the resentment seems to have grown strongest in the lower economic groups. In a 1964 poll, 34 per cent of all whites felt that the civil rights movement was seeking too much too fast. By 1965, 49 per cent felt that way, and by 1966, 85 per cent felt that way, even though two out of three whites agreed that the Negro was discriminated against. Almost four years ago, 61 per cent of an ethnic sample said that Negroes were getting a better break than their own immigrant fathers and grandfathers had received. Among whites earning less than $3,000 a year, 70 per cent believed that the war on poverty was designed for Negroes and would not help them, and these low-income whites were more alienated from society than any other group including Negroes. Almost two-thirds of the total white sample said that Negroes were discriminated against, but only 46 per cent of the poor felt that way. And while 46 per cent of the total white sample sympathized with Negro protests, only one-fourth of the poor sympathized.

National elections during the sixties carried other hints of this growing resentment. Hidden in the Johnson landslide of 1964 was the fact that the Democratic vote among ethnic groups in large cities was significantly down. Two years later, it had dropped off even further. The Polish Democratic vote in Ohio in 1966 was 45 per cent below the vote for John F. Kennedy in 1960.

So far, this resentment has found no workable political outlet. The sympathy most middle Americans have for Negro aspirations makes them turn away from candidates like George Wallace, and only 12 per cent of the *Newsweek* sample said the country would be better off with Wallace as President. The middle Americans are also too fragmented to keep the Negro down, even if they could find palatable ways of doing that. A sizeable minority does not think that the black man has as good a chance as they do, and in city after city they have combined with Negroes and upper class liberals—often in the face of conservative disunity—to elect moderates or liberal candidates. The number of Negroes in high political office has increased dramatically since 1966. It is impossible to say whether these trends will continue, because the Negro voting bloc may become fragmented itself. In the 1969 mayoralty campaign in Cleveland, Negro incumbent Carl Stokes backed a low-income housing project which was resisted by middle class Negroes, who said that the influx of poor blacks would ruin the neighborhood. In one of the two wards affected, both Stokes and his local candidate won. In the other, Stokes's local candidate lost and Stokes's white opponent for Mayor made a stronger showing than in any other Negro ward. But the middle American can expect to find few such allies in the black community.

For the moment, most middle Americans are left in an equivocal position. They are resentful of the Negro less because of the color of his skin than because they think the Negro is getting favors because of that color. Whether they are right or wrong—and there is hardly any evidence to suggest that they are right—that attitude is not bigotry. It is the same attitude that the black man in America has had for centuries, and the white man is no happier with it than the black man has been.

In the *Newsweek* poll and in comments to reporters, the same attitude was expressed toward many other groups in American society, by the angry and the merely resentful, the sympathetic and the hostile: "*They* are getting special favors, and I'm paying for them."

In one of the most lopsided answers in the poll, almost four out of five said that at least half the people on welfare were taking their money out of laziness. They were asked how many welfare recipients "could earn their own way if they really wanted to": 38 per cent said most could, another 41 per cent said about half could, 18 per cent said some could, and 2 per cent said hardly anybody could. Roughly

Q. HOW MANY PEOPLE ON WELFARE TODAY DO YOU THINK COULD EARN THEIR OWN WAY IF THEY REALLY WANTED TO—MOST OF THEM, ABOUT HALF, SOME, OR HARDLY ANYBODY?

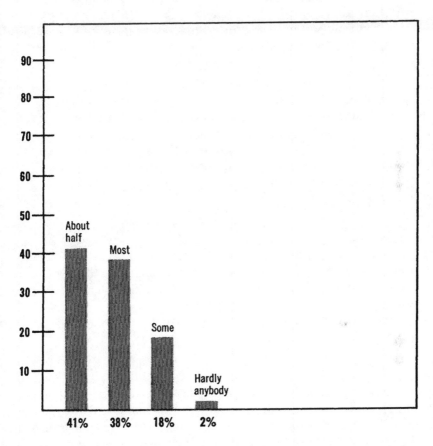

the same percentages held true for all groups in middle America, including the old, the young, the blue and white collar workers, those who thought the country was better than it used to be, and those who thought it was worse.

Yet, as reported in Chapter 3, the welfare chiselers seemed gray and far away. Forty-two per cent of the middle Americans listed welfare as one of the two or three most serious problems facing city people, but only 3 per cent listed it as a major problem in their own communities.

The same pattern appeared on questions concerning crime. When they were asked to list the nation's two or three most important problems, the middle Americans put crime seventh. When they were handed a list of problems facing people in cities and asked to pick the two or three most serious, almost two-thirds checked off crimes of violence, which topped their lists by a wide margin. Yet when they were asked whether violent crimes were a serious problem in their own communities, 42 per cent said it was fairly or very serious—and 56 per cent said it was not too serious or not serious at all. When they were asked to make up their own list of the main problems of their communities, they placed crime eighth.

When they listed the problems of the cities, the middle Americans put the use of drugs in third place, along with racial problems and welfare. Yet when they were asked how serious the problem of drug use by young people was in their own communities, 47 per cent said it was fairly or very serious, and 44 per cent said it was not too serious or not serious at all. And when they were asked to volunteer their own list of local problems, fewer than 4 per cent listed drugs at all.

Such answers raise two obvious possibilities: The middle Americans have encountered many of the things that incense them only second hand, in the newspapers and on television, or they are unwilling to admit that the problems exist close to home—or both.

In either case, from the middle American's perspective,

welfare cheats, criminals, and drug users tend to be shadowy figures in some unspecified other place. To this list of distant nemeses he adds college demonstrators, who by definition operate in some other place. Eighty-four per cent of the *Newsweek* sample said that college demonstrators had been treated too leniently, and 57 per cent said that such demonstrators had little or no justification.

Dr. S. I. Hayakawa, the president of San Francisco State College, who made himself a hero to millions of Americans by taking a firm stand with his student demonstrators, has said that the demonstrations are utterly incomprehensible to most Americans. "For most people, college is somewhere they always wanted to go but were too poor to," he says. "They can't understand why the hell people who have the privilege of going to college should try to shut it down—and why their professors should support them. They see college administrators without the courage to stand up to, punish, or expel students."

The middle American has a natural inclination to respect authority and to expect others to do the same, and he expressed these feelings strongly in the *Newsweek* poll. Almost two out of three said that the police have too little power in dealing with suspected criminals, and only 3 per cent thought they had too much power. Two-thirds felt that judges should be able to deny bail to a suspect if they thought the accused might commit a crime before he came to trial.

But the role of authority, like so much else in his society, is under attack right now, and authority does not seem to be putting up a very good fight. On the campuses, it often seems to be in a complete rout. In the courts, it seems to have thrown in with the troublemakers at the expense of their victims. On the police beat, it seems to be curbed by judges and politicians. Even in the nation's capital, the people Vice President Agnew called "an effete corps of impudent snobs" seem able to thumb their noses at it. Witnessing this apparent crumbling of authority through outside interference or abdication of its own responsibilities, the middle American

Q.   WHAT DO YOU THINK OF YOUNG PEOPLE AND COLLEGE
     STUDENTS WHO ARE INVOLVED IN DEMONSTRATIONS
     AND SIT-INS? ARE THEY COMPLETELY JUSTIFIED IN
     THEIR ACTIONS, IN LARGE PART JUSTIFIED, TO SOME
     DEGREE, VERY LITTLE, OR NOT AT ALL?

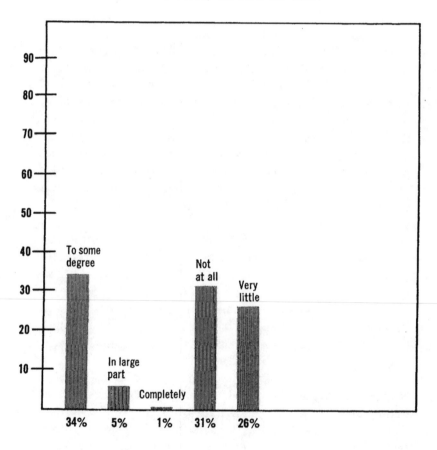

feels a special sense of betrayal. He himself paid the price of obedience, and now his tormentors are not only defying his protectors but getting away with it.

These twin themes of impotent and betrayed authority came out often in the middle Americans' conversations with *Newsweek* reporters.

"Why, people go right out in the street and call cops 'pigs' and get away with it," said a truck driver in Hayward, California. "Nowadays the kids don't live with the parents, the parents live with the kids. The church is just about getting lost. Things going on now disgust me so much I don't even want to think about it. I don't even read the paper except for the sports pages."

One Saturday afternoon in East Dallas, Texas, on a street lined with mimosa trees and modest GI homes, two brothers-in-law named Eddie Franks and Jack Woodlee discussed the state of the country while they sawed second-hand lumber for use in turning Franks' carport into a living room.

"I got cows in the bank and money out West," Jack Woodlee said, taking a bite of chewing tobacco and smiling ruefully. "Aw, hell, if the little people would stick together they could make the big boys get off their chairs and do something. But they won't.

"When taxes go up, they put them on us," Eddie Franks said. "When I got married twenty-two years ago, I made sixty cents an hour and my wife was jerking sodas. We're not much better off now. I get mad when I see these rich kids tearing up the schools and throwing away that opportunity. I had to work. I would have liked to go to college so I could have a job where I could sit up there all day and be clean."

"Ain't no way," said Woodlee. "When the unions give us a raise, the supermarkets go up two cents on canned goods, regular as a clock. And the politician doesn't help. He's only for himself."

"We shouldn't be spending all this money on foreign countries," said Franks. "All we get back is war."

"The rich man ought to have to pay taxes," said Wood-lee. "The country is supposed to be justice for all, not just for one or two, isn't it? But things ain't gonna get much better. The working man has always paid the load, fought the battles, and come home with less in his pocket."

One of the most galling aspects of the middle American's situation today is that he cannot quite make out how things got this way and at the same time feels powerless to do anything about it. In his own view of himself, he is the little man on the firing line, with the troublemakers somewhere out there in the shadows and the generals nowhere to be found. On top of that, the age-old panaceas for this kind of predicament no longer seem to work.

In times past, when sizeable numbers of Americans got upset about something they could not quite explain, they were inclined to fall back on the theory that there was a conspiracy afoot. Conspiracies have been trotted out to explain the annexation of Texas and the war with Mexico (a slaveholders' conspiracy), the economic plight of American farmers in the 1890's (an international money conspiracy), and the U.S. entry into World War I (a bankers' and munitions makers' conspiracy); more recently, various domestic problems have been laid to a Communist conspiracy. In their bitterness and bewilderment, some middle Americans of today also bring out the conspiracy theory. "The Supreme Court, the government, the church and the mass media have formed a conspiracy to take away all our freedom," a Louisiana man wrote *Newsweek*. But most middle Americans are unable to credit the idea of a conspiracy among such diverse groups, and for the moment they are left to curse the troublemakers and wait it out.

Even when the feeling of being victimized has not angered the middle Americans, it has troubled them. They may concede that there are injustices to be corrected, but they are deeply upset by the methods being used to correct them. Last fall, an insurance broker and former Marine leaned across a table in a Pittsburgh cocktail lounge and tried to unsnarl his complicated feelings about the Black Construction Coalition which was demonstrating for admission to the building trade unions.

"I don't mind people speaking out in meetings," he said. "But what I do mind is their exciting and inciting people, where there may be a rock or fire bomb thrown. They have conducted themselves well enough in their parades, but when the crowd breaks up it's uncontrollable to some extent, and at that point they begin to interfere with other people's rights. You don't know what to expect. My wife was coming downtown shopping yesterday, but when I learned that a demonstration was planned, I made her stay home."

He turned to the subject of college demonstrators. "These are the people who are supposedly going to be responsible later, so I pay attention to what they're doing," he said. "But authority has lost its ability to rule. You would have been expelled in my day for any number of violations many college students commit today." He mulled that over for a moment, then said, "But something must be wrong. Otherwise there wouldn't be all the dissension." He thought some more. "But again," he concluded, "these people are intruding on the rights of others."

Finally, he turned to the subject of taxes. "You have to generate more and more business simply to take home the same pay," he said. "The city has to raise more money to do the things society says it needs. So the landlords charge their tenants more, and the tenants charge the customers more, and it ends up hitting the individual square in the pocketbook—and we're the individuals. Where does it all stop? That's what people ask. Who can give us the answers to these things?"

5

THE MYTHS
OF
AFFLUENCE

*Do you know that we are the
only ones who pay taxes?*

—ERIC HOFFER

If the middle American's resentments can be traced back
to any one, specific source, that source probably is money.
The middle Americans range across a broad economic spectrum; their income runs from near poverty to near affluence,
and income alone is a slipshod measure of prosperity, because the cost of living varies at least 20 per cent from place
to place and a satisfactory income for a family of four is
meager or inadequate for a family of seven. Yet regardless
of where he stands on the economic scale, money is a source
of irritation to the middle American, and his irritation
springs from one central conviction: He thinks that while he
is breaking his back to make ends meet without outside help,

everybody else—the rich, the poor, and the Negro—is getting something for nothing.

The middle American, of course, feels cheated in other ways, too. He sometimes tends to think he is the only one sending his sons to Vietnam. He feels he obeys the laws while others break them and are turned loose to sin again. He feels he also obeys the moral laws of man and God, while others flaunt them and get away with it. But these resentments seem to be fueled by the central conviction that he does not have as much money as he deserves. He is making more than before, and he seems satisfied with the dollar amount coming in. In a 1949 poll, 50 per cent of all Americans said they were satisfied with their family income, and by 1969, 67 per cent were satisfied. But the money doesn't seem to go as far as it should. One of every four middle Americans in the *Newsweek* sample said that they were cutting down on the amount and quality of the things they buy. Perhaps more significantly, 44 per cent said that they were just managing to hold their own, and were no better off than they were five years ago. Almost eight out of ten said that federal taxes were too high (although it is hard to imagine a time when many people would say they are too low), and 59 per cent said that local taxes were too high. When they were asked to list the nation's most pressing problems, they put the high cost of living in third place and taxes fourth, and when they were asked to name the most pressing local problems, they put high taxes first and inflation second. What makes the middle American mad is not the amount of money he makes, which he considers an achievement, but the fact that it doesn't seem to bring him enough rewards. Again and again, he prefaces his other grievances with the claim that he is the honest working man who pays the taxes and gets nothing in return.

"We don't count, we are expendable—that is their attitude," Eric Hoffer shouts. "Do you know that we are the only ones who pay taxes? The rich don't pay taxes—we do."

It is impossible in a free economy to say just what consti-

Q. COMPARED WITH FIVE YEARS AGO, ARE YOU AND YOUR FAMILY ABLE TO BUY MORE AND BETTER THINGS THAN YOU DID THEN, ARE YOU HAVING TO CUT BACK ON WHAT YOU BUY, OR ARE YOU LIVING JUST ABOUT THE SAME AS YOU DID THEN?

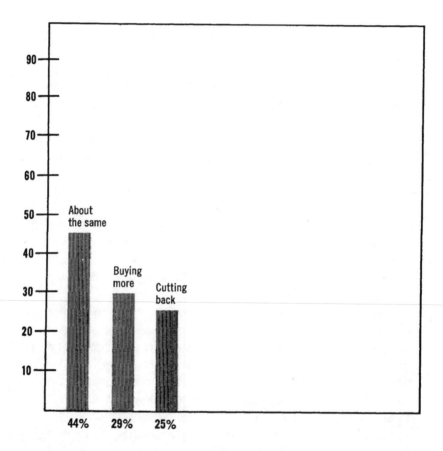

Q. WOULD YOU SAY THE TAXES YOU PAY TO THE FEDERAL
   GOVERNMENT IN WASHINGTON ARE TOO HIGH, TOO LOW,
   OR ABOUT RIGHT?

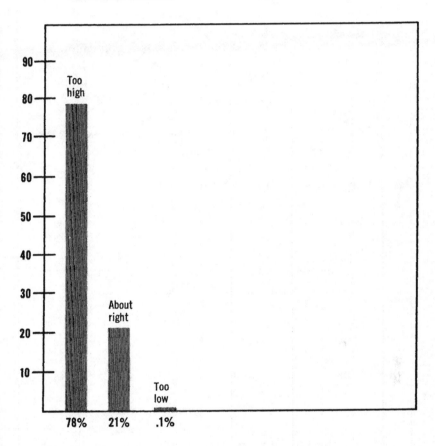

tutes a fair shake for the middle American, and sociologists disagree about the validity of his complaint. Some believe he is in fact carrying more of the load than he deserves.

"He finds his tax burden heavy, his neighborhood services poor, his national image tarnished, and his political clout diminishing," Robert Wood said. "This, too, is alienation." Daniel Moynihan writes: "We have established a Job Corps for the drop-out and a Peace Corps for the college graduate, but the plain fellow with a high school diploma, and his parents, have little to show from either the New Frontier or the Great Society. This—majority—group of Americans cannot but wonder what it is getting out of all the activity, and in particular has to be asking whether the government is playing favorites, or greasing squeaky wheels, or whatever."

Others point out that the middle American has come to take many of his own benefits for granted and exaggerates those that go to others. "As a matter of fact," says urbanologist Anthony Downs, "while welfare has gotten a lot of publicity, the fact is that the vast majority, more than 90 per cent, of the people on welfare are people who cannot work. They are old, sick, women. Secondly, this group has in fact been the beneficiary of many subsidies it doesn't recognize as such. The principal ones are the deductions from federal income tax for real estate taxes and interest on a home mortgage. That is just as much a subsidy as benefits to the poor, only they don't perceive it as such.

"This so-called forgotten American has been receiving. He has not been getting as much as the rich guy, but he gets more than the poor. In fact, though aid to the poor is very visible, this country's subsidies are slanted more toward the rich—things like the oil depletion allowance and all sorts of tax shelters."

"It's not accurate to say that Uncle Sam cares only for blacks," says Hyman Bookbinder of the American Jewish Committee. "More federal resources go to the middle class and the lower middle class, though they are not as visible."

Even Robert Wood believes that the middle American's

feeling of deprivation is partly the result of faulty vision. "This all comes at the end of a period when the major reforms for his benefit have been institutionalized, made rigid, and almost forgotten," he says. "Kennedy and Johnson responded to the needs of the blacks and the young and the poor. And the middle American forgot that he already had his. He is waiting for his turn to come, but he's already had it. He thinks it's his turn again, but he's at the back of the line and the line is a long one and he doesn't like it."

Whether his share is a fair one or not, many of the economic facts of life for the middle American are clear. The general economy has been booming. Since 1950, disposable personal income has gone from 207 billion dollars to 589 billion, and personal savings have gone from 13 to 41 billion. Personal outlays have increased from 194 to 548 billion, and per capita disposable income from $1,646 to $2,473. The incidence of poverty has been cut almost in half since 1959, from 20 per cent to 12 per cent.

The average American, who stands squarely in the middle of middle America, is the most prosperous average citizen in the world. If he is married, his median income is $9,144, and if he is single, it is $5,100. If his wife works, their median income is $10,686. If she doesn't work, their income is $8,215. In 1967, 40 per cent of all families fell into the $5,000 to $10,000 income bracket, while 22 percent earned $10,000 to $15,000.

The average American is married, has two children, and lives in a suburb or a metropolitan area. He is 44, his wife is 42, and they have been married twenty-one years. He works as a craftsman, foreman, or skilled worker in a private business, and he drives to work, either in his own car or in a car pool. Almost one-third of those in the $5,000 to $10,000 bracket, and half of those in the $10,000 to $15,000 bracket, own two cars. Both he and his wife are high school graduates, and he has served in one of the branches of the armed forces.

They bought their house within the last ten years, and the

house is twenty years old. Its value, as of 1967, was $14,600, and it has five rooms. It is in sound shape, with complete kitchen and bathroom facilities. They also have a telephone, at least one TV set, a clothes washer, and a radio. About one-fourth of the lower middle income group and 39 per cent of the upper middle income group own a color TV set. They have a little saved up: 35 per cent of those earning between $5,000 and $7,500 have savings of $1,000 to $5,000, and 54 per cent of those earning between $7,500 and $15,-000 have saved that much. They don't have a freezer, a dish washer, a clothes drier, or an air conditioner.

The picture of the average Negro is quite different. His median income is $5,360, and the U.S. Social Security Administration considers $5,080 as "near poverty" for a family of five. Only 35 per cent of all black families are in the $5,000 to $10,000 income bracket, and only 12 per cent earn between $10,000 and $15,000. Thirty-five per cent of all Negroes are below the poverty level, compared to 10 per cent of all whites.

The average American is aware that he makes more than the Negro, of course, and he also knows he is better off than the average man anywhere else, and he still feels he is being cheated. In terms of taxes, the figures do not seem to bear him out.

The middle Americans, including non-whites, comprise 63 per cent of the country's population, earn 60 per cent of its income, and pay 59.2 per cent of its taxes.

Those earning more than $15,000 comprise 12 per cent of the population, earn 30 per cent of the national income, and pay 26 per cent of the taxes.

Those earning less than $5,000 comprise 25 per cent of the population, earn 10 per cent of the income, and pay 14.7 per cent of the taxes.

Exact figures on Negroes do not exist, but they comprise 11 per cent of the population, earn about 6 per cent of the national income, and pay about 8 per cent of the taxes.

The great contaminating factor in all these means and

averages is the myth of affluence. America is a rich country, but it is not uniformly as rich as it thinks it is. For those at the bottom of the middle income range, the squeeze is sometimes acute.

"Here you have seven million white families whose gross income in 1967, the last year for which we have figures, was between five and seven thousand dollars," says Nicholas Kisburg, legislative director of the Teamsters' Joint Council 16 in New York. "Now that's one bloody step above welfare, and forty-four percent of these families had two or more wage-earners. So we are really not an affluent society so much as a hard-working society. Now what do you think that red neck thinks when he reads about a woman tearing down a welfare center? She may already be getting six thousand dollars a year. He doesn't read about the demoralized woman who is really living on sixty-six cents per person per day for food."

By the Labor Department's own standards, many of the middle Americans are not doing very well. The department maintains that an urban family today needs $5,915 a year to keep up a poor standard of living. A moderate standard of living takes $9,076 a year. The cost of a moderate standard of living in cities like New York and Boston, according to many experts, is over $10,000 a year, yet the median annual income in Irish South Boston is only $5,100. Half the families in the $5,000 to $10,000 bracket have two or more wage earners, and their prospects for improvement are not great. Only 6 per cent of them have gone past high school, and 43 per cent of them did not go past the eighth grade.

Inflation has also taken away many of the paper gains made over the past twenty years by the middle Americans, and sometimes it has obliterated them completely. From September, 1968 to April, 1969, weekly pay, measured in 1957 to 1958 dollars, rose $1.26—yet purchasing power dropped by $2.24, more than wiping out the gain. The inflation rate is now up to 7 per cent a year, and many economists think that it will remain high—and that as long as it remains high, purchasing power will continue to shrink. In recent years, inflation has eaten up about two-fifths of the middle American's pay increases. The small increase in his real prosperity has not chased the wolf from his door, but only backed him up a pace or two.

"Blue collar and white collar alike still live too near lay-offs, reductions, strikes, and plant relocation to be personally secure," Robert Wood has said.

"Psychologically, they're under as much pressure as ever," Arthur Ross, former Commissioner of Labor Statistics, has said.

Inflation has also thrown a psychological curve ball at the middle American: It is very hard to get rid of the idea that an income of, say, $8,000 a year is not a comfortable one, because when most Americans were forming their opinions about money, it was quite comfortable indeed.

Some government programs have also been applied inequably, and the middle American is the one who most feels the pinch when they are. Mitchell Sviridoff, a former aide to New York City Mayor John Lindsay who is now with the Ford Foundation, cites the cost of medical care in particular. "With the passage of Medicare and Medicaid," Sviridoff says, "we've driven up health costs to the point where they are beyond the reach of people who have to pay for them independently. Medicaid is now a poor people's program, even in the most progressive states. The people in between the poor, who benefit from the program, and the rich, who can afford to pay the higher health costs, are in a very, very real squeeze."

They are often in a housing squeeze, too. A Boston man last year raised his income to over $7,000 a year by working overtime, and as a result his rent in a government-controlled apartment was raised $28 a month—even though his actual increase in income could have been only a few dollars. College loan programs sometimes discriminate against the middle-income family as well. A widow in Chicago who earns

$7,000 a year doesn't qualify for a college loan for her child because the loans are limited to people on relief.

In other respects, the lower middle American's financial position has improved considerably. He owns more things than ever before. More than 60 per cent of those who earn between $6,000 and $7,500 a year own their own home, and almost all—89 per cent—own a car. He is more apt to receive insurance and health benefits from his employer. Nearly half of all union members now earn between $7,500 and $15,000 a year, and almost half of all union members are under 40 and can look forward to increasing earnings. Nearly half of all union members now live in the suburbs, and among those under 40, three-fourths live in the suburbs. The signs of labor's affluence are readily visible. On the last working day before a long weekend, the parking lots outside automobile plants in Flint, Michigan, are filled with cars with boats on their roofs. The walls of the Swan Boat Club, outside Detroit, are decorated with photographs of G. Mennen Williams' many campaigns. The pictures show Williams with club members, most of whom are blue collar workers. In the early pictures, the men are lean and only a few small boats can be seen in the background. As the photos get more recent, the men's stomachs grow larger, and their boats longer and more numerous.

In August, 1969, *The New York Times Magazine* reported on the life of a Queens family of five whose income was $13,140 a year—almost exactly the amount needed for a family of five to maintain a moderate standard of living in New York, according to the Bureau of Labor Statistics. The family income consisted of the husband's pay as a truck driver, $11,400, and the rent from a five-room apartment ($1,740) on the second floor of their house. The living style which such an income permitted seemed slightly better than moderate. They ate meat six nights a week, had their milk delivered, and owned an eight-year-old Buick (which originally cost $3,200), a dog (which cost $135), new, wall-to-wall carpeting in both the living and dining rooms, a wall oven, a color TV set ($750), and a number of smaller appliances, including an electric can opener. "Affluence?" the husband himself said. "I feel I'm making my fair share of it."

Labor officials have said that many union members also consider themselves affluent, partly because they like to think they are and partly because they are earning more than their fathers did. In fact, labor's position in American society has changed dramatically since the days when union leaders got their heads bloodied on picket lines. "Labor, to some extent, has become middle class," George Meany has said. "When you have no property, you don't have anything, you have nothing to lose by these radical actions. But when you become a person who has a home and has property, to some extent you become a conservative. And I would say to that extent labor has become conservative."

Whether it is a result of this increased conservatism or whether it is simply a protest against the increasing ravages of inflation, many middle Americans are up in arms over the high cost of living. In a poll taken in September 1969, members of Congress said that the rising cost of living was the dominant concern of the voters back home. "This is the greatest concern over the cost of living that I have found since I have been in public life," Senator George McGovern of South Dakota said. In many areas, the taxpayers are doing more than complaining. The leader of a taxpayer revolt in Michigan, Dr. John Carpovich, claims to have organized 30,000 workers in 19 counties to withhold their tax payments until property-owners are given tax relief. In Suffolk County, Long Island, in the elections of 1969, angry taxpayers in 25 towns rejected their proposed school budgets. "In California," Robert Finch, Secretary of Health, Education and Welfare, has said, "two-thirds of all school bonds are getting rejected, even in districts where no bond issue has ever been defeated.

"The guy sitting in his house just thinks there are a lot of programs that are not doing him any good. . . . We just have to persuade the public as a whole . . . that the so-called middle-class will also benefit if we can manage to improve the condition of the poor."

To many sociologists, such uprisings in middle America can only partly be explained in terms of economics, and only partly in terms of resentment at programs that seem to leave middle America out. A third, and possibly dominant, factor is that the growth of the American middle class has produced a revolution of rising expectations which parallels that of many black people in America. The middle American not only thinks he deserves more than he is getting, he wants more than he is getting, and many influences in American life have whetted that appetite. He is often told, directly and indirectly, that affluent Americans enjoy many material things. He has concluded from the figures on his pay check that he has reached the point of affluence, but many of the material things are not coming through the door. The system has not lived up to its part of the bargain.

Columnist Joseph Kraft has written that, as the working man's income has increased, he has abandoned beer for whiskey. "Their tastes and needs are up," says Hyman Bookbinder of the American Jewish Committee, "and have escalated more rapidly than the remarkable economic performance of the nation." "In terms of most measures, they are absolutely better off than in the past," Anthony Downs says. "So are the poor. But there is a gap between that and their own perception of their goals."

The middle American is technically affluent, says Irving M. Levine of the A.J.C., "but the affluence of the lower middle class American is a tenuous one, historically and even currently, and it does not allow him the comforts which the media say he deserves."

It is easy, and accurate, to make television and the other media villains in this drama of induced cravings. What television sells is rarely aimed at the middle American as a working man. There are no commercials for hammers, nails, lunch pails, diners, subways, blue collar shirts, or even pencils. One of the very few commercials for work equipment now being seen on TV is for an $8,000 automated typewriter for the busy executive's secretary, which is not the sort of thing the middle American is apt to have much use for. Judging by TV commercials, in fact, about the only working person in the country is the housewife, and she spends most of her working time trying to get clothes clean without wrecking her hands. Aside from shaving, the men hardly seem to work at all, and most TV ads are aimed at leisure time. Television peddles beer, cigars, cigarettes, new cars (often large ones), gasoline, cosmetics, perfume, hair dressing, ladies' clothes, airplane trips to exotic places, insurance, investment funds, banks, credit cards, loans, and, just for leavening, cereal, frozen food, and a little bread. Magazines sell about the same things, plus hard liquor. One astute letter-writer pointed out that the *Newsweek* article about the troubled American was interrupted by four pages of ads showing a handsome young couple smoking cigarettes in the country, a large and expensive car ("Something to believe in"), and a snappy-looking housewife sitting on a glistening new love seat with her arms full of newly bought packages.

Meanwhile, the news portions of these same outlets are filled with stories of rioting, pollution, and war. The entertainment portions feature assorted adventurers, cowboys, and detectives, and the few supposedly common people on television never seem to work and always seem to live in sumptuous surroundings.

Psychiatrist Bruno Bettelheim is one of those who blames the media for showing America only at its best and its worst, and he thinks television has helped brainwash the middle American into a totally unrealistic picture of life. "The middle class American today thinks of life as nice and easy, trying to shut out the realities of life, like the blood, sweat, and tears it takes to get along," he says. "This is the American myth, that the good life is easy to have. This, of course, is not so. But most middle class Americans are still living with this belief. When they finally realize how tough life really is, they are dissatisfied and bitter and resentful. It is not their fault but the fault of the entire society that has allowed this myth to go on living."

"Through television," says Anthony Downs, "we are encouraging on the consumption side things which are entirely inconsistent with the disciplines necessary for our production side. Look at what television advertising encourages: immediate gratification, do it now, buy it now, pay later, leisure time, hedonism. This is really serious, because the mark of the potential criminal is the inability to postpone gratification."

"The appetite and the sense of possibility generated by an affluent society," writes Irving Levine of the A.J.C., "create both the need and the assumption of wherewithal to consume conspicuously and repetitively. The average American is bombarded by the mass media message of abundance."

Yet there is a conundrum buried in these appraisals: If the middle American's myth is maintained by the mass media's message, who made the mass media maintain the myth except the middle American? No medium of communication has ever been so much at the mercy of public taste as American television. If it espouses immediate gratification, then immediate gratification is very probably what the public wants. Leonard Fein, Senior Research Associate of the Joint Center for Urban Studies, has noted that "society" has been coming in for a lot of criticism lately, while people seem to be absolved of all blame. With the addition of the middle American to the list of society's victims, two questions arise: Who is left to perpetrate all these evils, and who is left to correct them?

6

THE VOICES
OF
THE MIDDLE

They had no poet, and they died.

—ALEXANDER POPE

Traditionally, the common people of America never lacked for poets. Mark Twain, Carl Sandburg, Robert Frost and Willa Cather celebrated the small-town people of the Mississippi, the butchers of Chicago, and the plain farmers of New England and the Southwest. Popular songs reflected the lives and values of everyday people, and popular humorists like George Ade, and Will Rogers, and entertainers like Fibber McGee and Molly assumed kinship with the average man. Even in America's least realistic art, the movies, actors like Gary Cooper and James Stewart made heroes out of simple men who were called to do great deeds, and from the Revolution until well after World War II, the common clay was assumed to be the stuff of most American art, high or low. But gradually, over the course of the past twenty years, the common people have disappeared from America's own culture. They are no longer seen in the most respectable novels or movies. They rarely appear on television, and their values are not to be found in most popular songs. They have not vanished completely. In 1966, while the Beatles sang of "Nowhere Man" and Simon and Garfunkel sang of "The Sounds of Silence," the number-one record in the country was "The Ballad of the Green Berets." In 1968, *The Graduate* was the most popular movie, but the second most popular was John Wayne's *The Green Berets*. But most of the common folk who do appear in movies and songs now tend to be sad and forgotten, like Eleanor Rigby, who went out wearing a face that she kept in a jar by the door and was buried along with her name. In American culture today, the common man is like the buffalo of the Great Plains—not quite but almost extinct.

The same sort of diminution has afflicted the place which the common people have always regarded with the most fondness, the American small town. When the country was new, its most sophisticated statesman, Thomas Jefferson, wrote that "The small landholders are the most precious part of a state." "I think our governments will remain virtuous for many centuries; as long as they remain chiefly agricultural," he wrote. "And this will be as long as there shall be vacant lands in any part of America. When they get piled upon one another in large cities, as in Europe, they will become corrupt as in Europe, and go to eating one another as they do there." Throughout their short history, Americans have bestowed more love on their out-of-the-way places than on their big cities, even while they were packing to go somewhere else or, once there, noting sadly that you can't go home again. "I have fallen in love with American names," wrote Stephen Vincent Benét. "The sharp names that never get fat/The snakeskin-titles of mining-claims,/The plumed war-bonnet of Medicine Hat/Tucson and Deadwood and Lost Mule Flat."

But gradually, after World War II, the small places began to disappear or take on the look of museums. Sometimes they grew to be large cities, like Tucson, and sometimes, like Medicine Hat, they simply withered away. The small towns that were left seemed, thanks to television, to be at once connected with the greater world and cut off from it. In 1963, Leslie Hanscom reported in *Newsweek* on a little town in Iowa, "a place so small that nobody is one too many; where the pillars of government all have faces and first names." "Keosauqua can hardly avoid belonging to the great world," he wrote, "but the cost of membership may be far too high. By an irony of history, the world it belongs to seems to have no place for the American small town."

In the space of twenty or thirty years, America has thus lopped both the common people and the small town from its imagination. In the broadest sense, the common man had been forgotten by both poets and politicians. Now he is making a comeback. But like many comebacks, it is strained, and there is a lot of question whether it is legitimate or trumped up and how long it will last.

In their comeback, the middle Americans have so far produced no poets and few genuine heroes. In New York, while they were deciding between Mario Procaccino and John Marchi for mayor, the rich, the liberals, and the blacks got together and re-elected a Yale man. On the national scene, George Wallace probably talks the middle Americans' language better than anybody, but the middle Americans don't care for much of what he says. The President speaks to the middle Americans' sympathies, but he was a wealthy Wall Street lawyer when he was elected, and his personal style is nearer Thomas Dewey's than Harry Truman's. The Vice President is of Greek origin and probably says more things that the middle American likes to hear than anybody on the political scene; but with his immaculate clothes, erect bearing, and elegant language, he does not seem a man of the common people, not a man who would willingly take off his jacket, but one who came from the common people, graduated, and is still loyal to his alma mater.

Instead of leaders and heroes, the middle American today is represented by a loose array of spokesmen. Some are well known, some are little known, some are intellectuals, some are untutored, some are of the political right, some are of the left, some work in middle America, and some only study it. Unlike the leaders of the blacks or the young, these spokesmen have few common bonds. They hold no meetings, and there are no posters of them on middle America's walls. But as a group, they provide the only informed glimpse of middle America's thinking available outside of polls and interviews, and although they disagree on many particulars, they are in substantial agreement about middle America's basic fears and resentments. Their views are worth listening to.

Paul Deac is a short, dark-haired, vehement man with a missing cartilage in his nose, an injury which he attributes to boxing. His father was a Baptist minister in Warren, Ohio, and Deac went to Warren's public schools, then emigrated from middle America to the Sorbonne, where he lived with a French senator whom his father had befriended. He spent the better part of twelve years in France, became a correspondent for the Anglo-American News Agency and late in the 1930's went to work as a reporter for the Chicago *American*. In 1941 he moved over to the Detroit *Free Press* and was put in charge of building circulation among ethnic readers, and much of his time ever since has been spent working with ethnic groups. He was rejected by the army during World War II and after that, took a job on the French desk of the International News Service in New York, then worked for a Long Island radio station and the Voice of America. While there, he fed Senator Joseph McCarthy information on people he suspected were subversives, and although he later decided that McCarthy's tactics were unfair, the episode led to his ouster from the Voice of America in 1953. He moved to Washington, where he worked for suburban papers and the American Trucking Association, and in 1956 he helped organize The Confederation of American Ethnic Groups. He became its salaried national Executive Vice President.

Deac is a man who wears his resentments on his sleeve, and today he is angry about white liberals, black favoritism, black crime, ethnic neglect, and both political parties. "New York liberals are dogs," he says. "The burning of cities, law-lessness, permissiveness in our colleges, is pushed as a weap-on by progressive liberals to bring the nation to its knees so that they can rule, because that's what's wanted—to rule, not govern. I can't see these people [the ethnic groups] go-ing right, but they're being pushed that way. We do respect the right to dissent, but not to the point of insurrection. We're moderates.

"Nixon has said he would be the champion of the forgot-ten man," Deac says. "We're still waiting. After one year, Nixon is still on the outside looking in. Nixon, like Kennedy and Johnson, has reiterated the need for preferential treat-ment for Negroes, Mexican Americans, and Puerto Ricans. But he has failed so far to include the ethnic groups, and the same resentment is building up against him as it did against the Democrats. This is not criticism but a statement of fact. We're not going back to the liberal Democrats. They took our vote and shut us off from the benefits. Unless the GOP gives due consideration, they can't make any headway. We're not going to exchange one master for another. So Wallace may be the only answer."

Deac is also upset at some ethnic Congressmen who, in his eyes, are giving blacks preferential treatment, notably Representative Brademas of Indiana, Representative Dingell of Michigan, and Representative Pucinski of Illinois; he complains about waiting two or three hours to see Pucinski while a couple of Negroes were ushered in ahead of him. "We're not against Negroes," he says. "We work with them. We're against Negro and white militants who have gone be-yond the right of dissent, who are insurrectionists. I cannot emphasize too strongly we're not against giving Negroes the break they deserve. We're for cooperation, not conflict. We know they've been discriminated against. But two wrongs don't make a right. If he gets preferential treatment, that's bad."

Deac thinks the ethnic groups are suffering from an economic squeeze, and he says they are totally alienated by the changing moral standards. "They're 100 per cent against permissiveness," he says. "Not $99\frac{44}{100}$ per cent, but 100 per cent. I know a lot of families who, if their kid came home with long hair, they'd chase him right out." Deac himself has a consultant who wears a neat, clean beard. The man's appearance at board meetings so disturbed some of the membership that Deac now keeps him away from meetings.

In conversation, Deac frequently pictures himself and other ethnic leaders as reasonable people with an angry dog on a weak leash: They may be knocked aside if their counsel is not heeded by outsiders. Deac himself claims to be a Democrat, and a liberal one. He says The Ethnic Foundation took a survey in several cities to determine the size of the ethnic vote for Wallace, and came up with a figure of two million. "We hope Nixon keeps his promises so this trend won't be accelerated," he says. "But the pot is boiling. We spend millions and the Negroes get everything and we get nothing. We are not against tending to the needs of the black poor. If we were, the civil rights laws and many other liberal laws couldn't have been passed. We're against preferential treatment. No one, including ourselves, is entitled to preferential treatment. We preach that the poor Negro is in the same boat as poor whites and we don't have to preach much. But when your wife is raped, your home is broken into, this is all rubbed out.

"We're at the crossroads. We counsel moderation, but when they have to eat, when they're deprived of their life savings and physically attacked and someone comes offering counsel and moderation, they turn on you and tell you to get out. Maybe we do need a good dictator," he concludes.

Representative Roman Pucinski of Chicago was born in Buffalo, New York, in 1919, and his family moved to Chicago when he was three. He graduated from Northwestern and John Marshall Law School and was a reporter for the Chicago *Sun-Times* for twenty years. During World War II, he enlisted in the Army Air Force as a private and came out a captain. He led his bomber group on the first B-29 raid over Tokyo, flew a total of forty-eight missions over Japan, and was awarded the Distinguished Flying Cross and Air Medal with clusters. Pucinski went to Congress from a polyglot district in 1959 and has been there ever since, and he is considered a regular in Mayor Daley's Congressional delegation. He wears his silver hair slightly long and is a natty dresser, and during his reporting days he was virtually the only member of the Chicago press corps to drive a Cadillac. He is National Chairman of the Polish-American Committee on Equality, and he makes it a practice to stand on a street corner at least an hour every Saturday, talking to his constituents. "These people today are in revolt," he says.

"The middle-income American today is earning more and enjoying it less," Pucinski says. "The country was unprepared for ten years of sustained prosperity. The increase in taxes leaves a guy with no more despite raises. They get raises their wives never see because so much is taken out of their check. They're in revolt against taxes. They don't want to leave the city, but they're being forced into it. We insist on driving a white American into the ground before we can give him any help. And we're getting to the place where a middle American won't be able to buy a house. We're driving him right out of the home-buying market.

"And they tell me they just don't recognize their kids. They say it almost apologetically. They say, 'I don't know what they're teaching these kids in college.' It's more disillusionment and heartbreak than anger. But they become very angry when they talk about the media. There's a sizeable school of thought that if the media were to block out some of the stuff they show or print, it would go away. They don't like to see so much time and space devoted to extremists. They're angrier with the TV than with the President or anyone else. If the silent majority did nothing else, it has made the media more sophisticated than they were in the sixties, when they were so hep on dissent and became chroniclers not of news but of dissent.

"Nothing has them more depressed than Vietnam," Pucinski says. "Vietnam, the draft, have a great impact on over-all happiness. It's a cloud. It takes the pleasure out of good times, the two cars, the new furniture, the home. They come up to me and say, 'Congressman, I finally worked my way up'—and then they mention their boy's going to Vietnam. There's a big pacifist drive. It's getting hard to stir them in defense of great national causes. Most are saying, 'Live and let live.' They hope if they hope hard enough, it'll go away.

"They also know integration has to come," Pucinski says, "but their big concern is property values. These second generation people inherit from their parents a reverence for their home. The Polish have a word, *grunt*: a base, a foundation. A lot of them want reconciliation with the blacks, but then there comes a shoot-out with the Panthers. . . . And they can't understand why the investigations afterward seem to concentrate on the role of the police.

"There's a trend against hiding behind the Constitution, all the turmoil in the country, but there's no shift to the right on social issues. They took better vacations than ever before this year, and despite all the complaining, when you press them they'll say that on the whole it's pretty good. We've entered an era of the moderates. Middle America, I think, has made its point. Extremists on both sides are running for shelter. There's disenchantment in middle America with the New Left as represented by McGovern, McCarthy, and those they feel condone street violence—like Goldberg defending the Black Panthers. Politically, they're not too happy with Nixon—in fact, there's bitter disappointment with Nixon. But Nixon is benefitting from the same phenomenon we saw in the closing days of the 1968 campaign, when Muskie caught on and helped carry Humphrey with a lot of these people. There's even a joke among the political people in my district: 'In '72, it's going to be Agnew and Nixon.' "

Paul Jacobs is a short, egg-bald radical who has been, at various times, an apprentice diamond merchant in New York, a leftist radical (later a Trotskyite) at the University of Minnesota, an ILGWU organizer in Pennsylvania, New York and the South, an Army Air Force sergeant, a member of the Labor Division of the American Jewish Committee in New York, a CIO representative in California, and, finally, since 1954, a writer in San Francisco. He was born into a Jewish family in middle America, but his familiarity with it has fluctuated over the years.

"I worked with middle America when I was a union organizer, and I didn't understand very much about it at the time," Jacobs says. "When I started writing, once more I had to deal with middle America and the responses of middle America to the things I believe in. I found myself very much an outsider. The views I have are certainly not the views of middle America.

"The middle Americans believe that the blacks are getting too much. One of the comments you always hear is, 'You gotta be a nigger to get a job these days.' America's perception of the race problem is so skewed, so awry, so distorted, it reflects on every other problem in American society. Middle America is disgruntled and feels it isn't getting its fair share. It feels it has to pay high taxes which are then used to support, in the view of middle America, people on relief who are laying around, drinking wine, having kids, and not working.

"And middle America feels threatened on the question of

housing. Here these people busted their ass working for their house, and they've got an investment in their house, and then the goddam coons or the goddam Mexicans or some goddam other people are going to come in and drive the property value down. It's awfully difficult to go and explain to them that that doesn't happen. On certain basic questions affecting the future of the society, there ought to be some attempt to explain to middle America the dangers that we're all facing. The race question—that's been totally neglected. No explanation has been made to middle America. I understand why the workers feel threatened by black demands for jobs, because they foresee facing unemployment. No one tried to explain what the real issues are, what the real problems are, and that's generally true of all the problems we confront.

"Their frustration is also coupled to the Vietnam situation. Americans have been so conditioned to believe we're all powerful. Suddenly they have to confront a situation in which a bunch of half-naked brown guys, little bitty ones running around in sneakers, are beating the shit out of those good American boys with crew cuts and heavy, hobnailed boots and the latest technology.

"Then, too, the young and the intellectuals don't respect middle America. One reason they don't respect them is they don't know anything about middle Americans. What you have are really sharp separations in modes of life. The middle American sees some hippie kid walking down the street wearing a jacket made out of an American flag and he goes up the wall. That's a total assault on what he believes to be correct. Here is middle America working hard, eight hours a day, going bowling on Wednesday night, putting on his shirt with the company name on the back and his name on the pocket—in middle America, the name on the shirt pocket is always 'Chick'—and here's this goddam hippie kid laying around. Not only is he not working, he's *enjoying* not working.

"They're also fragmented. In a sense, we really aren't a unified country so much as a congeries of countries. On the other hand, they're held together by a certain set of common values: a commitment to God, a commitment to religion, a commitment to patriotism, a commitment to work, a commitment to a belief in racial superiority. These are notions which are not held by the rest of America.

"I don't think middle America has any more excessive material expectations than anyone else, but that's one of the most disheartening aspects of American society. From the time a child is born, he is trained to look at material aspects of affluence as being the most important thing in the world. Middle America is no more guilty than the rest. But the rich don't have to be concerned because they've got it already, and the poor don't have any expectations about ever getting it. It's this poor bastard in the middle who thinks somehow he's going to make it. He's tantalized by everything he sees on television, in the media, in the society around him, by an affluence he can't ever achieve. Obviously, there's going to build up a tremendous amount of frustration.

"You know, one of the things that got me thinking about them again was George Wallace," Jacobs says. "He was the only person in the Presidential campaign who really talked about issues that troubled people. A good number of liberals and radicals totally misunderstood the nature of the Wallace constituency. Instead of directing ourselves to those people, we drove a wedge between us. Wallace had the wrong answers, he had the wrong explanations about why they felt the way they did, but he certainly talked about things that were troubling people."

Eric Hoffer is the common man's prima donna. Bull-necked and bellicose at 69, his voice roars, his heavy hands beat the table, and ideas pop from him in short, powerful bursts, like body punches. Born in New York, he was blinded in a fall at 7, regained his sight at 15, traveled to California at 18, worked in a factory, spent about twenty years roaming the West Coast with the Oakies, then spent the next twenty-five years working as a longshoreman in San Francisco and writing books of essays and philosophy. Today, Hoffer is retired, and he spends his time walking six miles a day, talking to people in the streets, and holding forth to students, civil servants, and assorted visitors in a cramped room in the political science department at the University of California at Berkeley.

Hoffer is a man of passionate hates. He hates criminals and "bushy-headed, brutalizing Negro hoodlums." He hates the rich tax-dodgers and their offspring, the "rich punks." He hates today's youth, which is "slovenly and stoned . . . on its way to the ashcan." His opinion of the common man is not what it used to be, either. Hoffer calls him "meek, cowardly, and passive." But he loves the country.

One afternoon early in 1970, Hoffer sat in his small office and, speaking for middle America in the common "we," offered answers to the questions of a group of visiting administrators from the Housing and Urban Development, Health, Education and Welfare, and Justice departments.

"The Negroes say they created the wealth of this country," Hoffer bellowed. "The hell they did. While they were dragging their asses around picking cotton, my ancestors were working eighty hours a week in the factories and mills. They were creating the goddam wealth of this country, and you're not going to inject us with any sense of guilt about the Negro. We don't feel guilty, because our white face didn't give us any advantage, goddamit. What advantage did our white face give us, goddamit? The Lindsays, the Percys, the Kerners feel guilty, and I'll tell you why. They live in exclusive neighborhoods. Send their children to exclusive schools. Use every tax loophole there is. And then they come to us and tell us we should integrate our schools, integrate our houses, and pay our taxes to help the poor. They feel guilty because of this hypocrisy.

"But there is no sense of guilt in eighty per cent of the population, and you can talk from here till Doomsday and you ain't gonna make us feel guilty. If you are a Negro and you can read and write, you can do anything you want. An alibi is a million times more valuable than achievement. Negroes use discrimination as an alibi. Do you think they will give up their alibi—their freedom to fail? Never!"

Hoffer was asked what effects he thought the black revolution had had.

"The introduction of the Negro into our stream of life has reversed the amalgamation in the melting pot," he said. "The ethnic groups that were more or less amalgamated are crystalizing out of the goddam amalgam. Everywhere you look, you see ethnic groups seceding from America."

He was asked his opinion of black study programs.

"What business have we got giving special studies to anybody?" he demanded. "If you don't want to be an American, that's just too bad for you."

He was asked about law and order and crime in the streets.

"This is something I worry about, how to clean up the city, how to eliminate fear from the cities," Hoffer said. "Our cities are packed with bushy-headed, brutalizing Negro hoodlums. Our cities are packed with people unfit to live in cities. I'm a pessimist. I'm frightened. I'm worried because I love this country. You always think the things you hate are strong and the things you love are brittle.

"You need order in order to have a civilized society. Fear and freedom are mutually exclusive. Right now you are not living in a free society. The choice we have is between two non-free societies. One, the society we have now, with all the constitutional guarantees of individual freedom and all these goddam things, and yet we cannot control these willful savages, these beasts masquerading as men who mug us, rob us, who do anything they want with us. This is one kind of non-free society. The other is a dictatorship, where you have no freedom to say what you want but the streets are safe all the time. And I'll bet you eighty per cent of the people if they could choose would vote for a dictatorship.

We have no alternative unless we are ready to put our life on the line. Where if somebody says, 'Give me your wallet,' you say, 'Fuck you, come and get it and die trying.' When he goes to the bank and asks for the money and the girl says, 'The hell I will, let him shoot me.' If you do that, you're going to survive, you're going to have an orderly society. If all the people are afraid and you expect the police to do everything for you, and when the policeman gets a little mad you accuse him of police brutality . . . if I was a policeman, I wouldn't help nobody. It used to be everybody was his own policeman. Nobody fights any more. We are all civilized, all ready for the slaughter. Anybody can kill us. We aren't more violent, we are less violent."

Hoffer was asked what he thought of the gulf between the rich and the intellectuals, on one hand, and the middle American, on the other. "The rich and the poor are being radicalized and we are right in the middle," Hoffer said. "We are doing most of the work, paying most of the taxes, working like hell to make ends meet, and we can't afford to send our kids to college. We are paying for the college education of the rich punks whose parents are dodging taxes by using every loophole that exists. The SDS revolution is subsidized by the rich. But in an affluent society, richness loses its meaning. To feel really rich, you need lots of poor people around you."

He was asked what he blamed for all this trouble.

"I'm blaming everything on television," Hoffer said. "I can't prove it. But if I were to activate the silent eighty per cent of the American people, I would have a symbolic act. At twelve o'clock all the sirens would blow, and when they stopped, we'd open all the windows and throw the television sets into the streets. This would be a declaration of independence. Everybody sits in front of his TV and eats his TV dinner, and you can't help your brother because you have to get home to watch a program at seven o'clock. TV has made the majority meek, cowardly, and passive. It's because of this that the violent minority escalates."

Somebody asked what Hoffer thought of the young.

"The young are slovenly and stoned, decked out in nightmarish masquerade on its way to the ashcan," Hoffer said. "You go down on Telegraph Avenue and you'll see how Calcutta came to Berkeley. This is what frightens me, the young generation.

"These new one-semester intellectuals think anyone who says anything good about this country is simple-minded," Hoffer added. "The password is to run down this country. Then you're sophisticated. This is a goddam good country."

Saul Alinsky was trained as a sociologist and criminologist at the University of Chicago in the early 1930's and has spent most of his life trying to get a piece of the action for various minority groups. He has organized stockyard workers in Chicago, the black poor of Rochester, and the Mexican-American poor of California (Cesar Chavez, the leader of the grape pickers' boycott, studied under Alinsky). Today, Alinsky's self-appointed task is to get the white majority back into the mainstream.

Alinsky sees the middle American as a person who pinned his hopes on a formula that is now outdated. In his book *Reveille for Radicals*, published in 1946 and recently revised, he wrote that the middle Americans "cast their lot with the haves, as—with a few burning individual exceptions—the middle class always does. They moved into the nightfall of success, and the dreams of achievement which make men fight were replaced by the restless nightmares of fear: fear of change, fear of losing material possessions. Today, they are part of the city's establishment and are desperately trying to keep their community unchanged. . . .

"I believe that white Americans welcome the present race violence and that under the surface reactions of horror and shock is very deep relief. Now white Americans are back in the familiar jungle. Now they can have a confrontation, because they think they know the answer to violence, and the answer is force. . . . Now they no longer have to talk or think about injustice, guilt, or the immorality of racism. Now it is simple: 'Law and order must be upheld before we get around to anything else. . . .'

"The chasm between the people and their political representatives has widened to a terrifying degree. . . . They are even more alienated from the scene than the poor, because what they had after they got it was not the good life; they do not know where to go, they lack any compass or direction, so they founder and are frightened. The poor at least have a compass, a direction, and a purpose because, regardless of what anyone says to them, getting that bank account, that color-TV, that house in the suburbs, and two cars is happiness."

"Let's face it," Alinsky says. "The middle class represents four-fifths of this country's population. If you took every minority group in this country and somehow got them together, they still wouldn't have the numbers to change things. The middle class has the numbers, but they feel too cut off from the entire society to try and change things. Someone has got to show them how to get a voice in this country. It comes through organization.

"Generally, there has been a turning away from everything and everyone by the middle class. They have the feeling of being lost, a feeling that there is no one to turn to, a feeling that they don't have anyone to speak for them.

"The white middle class is suffering from mass schizophrenia. You always hear the expression 'not getting involved.' Everything is so goddamed confused now. You've got an automated form of society, experts for everything and yet no one knows what to do about anything. On top of that, the middle class sees a government that doesn't speak for them or represent them. The United States Senate is one-third millionaires and two-thirds well on their way. They feel pretty well locked out of that scene.

"When you have a population so forlorn and turning away

from everything, you have a situation where huge vacuums develop. It's in these types of vacuums that a Hitler can come in, a demagogue. De Tocqueville in 1835 said the one thing that really will finish democracy is if you ever get a situation where the people feel impotent, where they feel they have nothing whatever to say about their lives. Then the whole democratic thing will collapse and finally in their desperation and frustration, they will turn and throw themselves at the feet of a single dictator. The final appeal of a demagogue is always 'Follow me and I'll give you answers.' "

Mayor Sam Yorty of Los Angeles has been around a long time. During the depression years, he was an outspoken liberal. In the forties, he became vocally anti-communist. In the early sixties, he was considered the black man's friend. Today, Yorty talks about law and order. "He is a very sensitive politician," says one of his critics.

Yorty was elected to the State Assembly in 1936 from an ultra-liberal district, and pleased his constituents by fighting for a 30-hour work week and freedom for Tom Mooney, a labor leader involved in the Preparedness Day bombing. In 1940, he led the formation of the state's Un-American Activities Committee and served as its chairman. He has tasted political defeat often since then. He lost a race for the U.S. Senate in the early forties, lost twice more in Senate bids, and lost twice running for Mayor. When he won on his third try, in 1961, he got 60 per cent of the black vote, even though he had supported Nixon against Kennedy in 1960. During the campaign, he convinced the black community that he would rein in hard-line police chief William Parker. Two days after the election, Yorty had a closed-door meeting with Parker. Nobody knows what was said, but Yorty rarely criticized Parker again. But he did appoint blacks to city commissions, the first such appointments in the city's history. Yorty has a reputation for effusiveness, and, like

Mario Procaccino, his lack of smoothness sometimes helps him with voters. "I like him because he's so emotional," a Queens housewife said of Procaccino. "Any tears he sheds, you know he has heart. He doesn't fear to shed them and they bring the people closer to him." "Personally, I like the way he shoots of his mouth too much," a white-haired man said of Yorty recently. "He'll do a better job for me than the other guy."

Yorty's last opponent for Mayor was Thomas Bradley, a Negro who, until the last minute, had looked like a clear-cut winner. The campaign was grueling and, in the opinion of some observers, rough. Yorty hit hard on the theme of law and order, and Democrats accused him of blatantly playing on voters' fears of black crime and black riots. When it was all over, Yorty had won by a narrow margin, but he denies that he played on racial fears to do it.

"I consider myself a liberal," Yorty says. "They don't know that I integrated city government eight years ago and that three of the five police commissioners—and they are the ones who run the police department—are a minority, a Jew, a Negro, and a Mexican. And the same with the Civil Service Commission. I've always been for fair law enforcement, but the Supreme Court has swung the balance over on the side of the criminal. On race, I'm a liberal. The press is distorted, biased, anti-western." But Yorty concedes that many people in Los Angeles may be unaware that he is a liberal on race. "This city's population has grown by half the size of San Francisco since I've been Mayor, a good deal of them from the South," he says. "Now they don't know my record on race, sure." He shrugs.

In June of 1969, a former policeman named Charles Stenvig, known to most people as Charlie, was elected Mayor of Minneapolis, Stenvig had run on a promise "To take the handcuffs off the police." "As your mayor," he pledged, "I wouldn't let a few hoodlums dictate the policies for the majority of the hard-working, law-abiding citizens of Minneapolis." His opponent, Republican Daniel Cohen, accused him of peddling "a thinly veiled kind of racism," but Stenvig hammered away at the question of decency. "Human relations can be summed up in one saying: the Golden Rule," he said during a campaign speech. He won with 62 per cent of the votes, sweeping eleven of the city's thirteen wards. "God," he announced in his inauguration speech, "is going to be my principal adviser."

If God is Stenvig's principal adviser, He may also be the only one who knows what to make of Stenvig's election.

On the nights of August 12 and 13, two months after the election, there was a confrontation between police and some of Minneapolis' small Negro population in the city's ghetto. R. Hopkins Holmberg, Fifth District (Minneapolis) Democratic leader, criticized the "swarming behavior" of the police. "Charlie said he would take the handcuffs off the police," Holmberg said, "and that's what's happening. The force has a tendency to get out of hand once in a while, and Charlie was a spokesman for this kind of thing."

"It's anti-establishment," the research director for Stenvig's opponent said of Stenvig's appeal during the campaign. "Charie offers simple answers to a society that has become extremely complex. Who the hell can knock the Golden Rule?"

"It was a middle class revolt," says Paul Helm, who runs a radio talk show in Minneapolis and was an early and vocal supporter of Stenvig. Until two years ago, Helm settled auto insurance claims for a living. Then he appeared on a radio program, lambasted welfare chiselers, police handcuffers, courts, and college pinkos, and earned his own program. "You give me a year's dictatorship and I'll reduce the crime rate eighty per cent," Helm says. "It wouldn't be pretty. But it would be effective."

"It was the first time people had a chance to kick the millionaires in the teeth," he says of Stenvig's election. "All

I did was give voice to a lot of things people had begun to feel. They'd just about had it on almost everything. Stenvig talked to them in their own language. They were sick of the intellectuals who say we're simplistic. An intellectual is a guy who took three courses in college and read three books. They want to complicate everything. The people were sick and tired of the bleeding hearts who have more sympathy for the criminal than they have for the victim."

"There is no hostility in him," says Arthur Naftalin, Stenvig's predecessor, a Democrat, and a widely respected political scientist and urban affairs specialist at the University of Minnesota. "His initial response to the little guy was authentic. Charlie's way of putting things is a kind of shorthand way to say a lot of things to a lot of people. They can read into it what they want to."

"Stenvig came on like a beleaguered policeman, the only one standing up for their old values," says Dr. William Wright, a history professor at the University of Minnesota.

"Stenvig told those rich guys downtown to go suck a lemon," says an auto mechanic in Minneapolis.

Charles Stenvig is 42 years old, a Methodist of Norwegian stock and the son of a telephone company employee. He went to Roosevelt High School, served in the Army, and graduated from Augsburg College, which he attended on the G.I. bill in 1951. He and his wife Audrey were married after his graduation, and they live in a modest ranch house in a middle class neighborhood on the northwest side of Minneapolis, near the airport. Stenvig joined the police force as a patrolman, became a detective in 1964, and was elected President of the Police Federation. When Mayor Naftalin announced that he was not going to run for reelection, people started urging Stenvig to enter the race, and he agreed. In the non-partisan run-off, he beat a far more conservative City Councilman who had the backing of the Central Labor Union and civic leaders in both parties. Stenvig's margin was two to one.

In the mayoralty election, Stenvig's opponent, Daniel

Cohen, was the son of a Minneapolis investment banker. Cohen went to private school in Minneapolis, Stanford University, and Harvard Law School, and he and his wife, Gail, live in a 50-year-old house in Kenwood, a fashionable area of the city on the southwest side. He is a lawyer and since 1965 has been President of the Minneapolis City Council. One of Stenvig's more popular campaign lines was the promise "to bring government back to the citizens of Minneapolis and away from the influence of the golden West out there in Wayzata," a fashionable suburb.

Since Stenvig's election, there has been general but subdued approval of his administration, mixed with general but subdued criticism of his appointments. "They're mostly just average working people," Stenvig himself says. His Administrative Deputy is Tom Ogdahl, who, as a young man, had a reputation as a street fighter. Since his appointment, he showed up at work one morning with a split lip, and said that there had been a disagreement but that he hadn't fought back. As a member of the Minneapolis Commission on Human Relations, Stenvig appointed Antonio G. Felicetta, a Teamsters Union vice president. In his first press conference after his appointment, Felicetta lost no time laying out his theoretical framework. "I'm not going to take any bullshit," he said. "If there are grievances, I sure as hell would want to see them taken care of. But I sure as hell wouldn't want to give 'em half my goddam pay check when I'm working and they're sitting on their asses. Don't expect me to get raped by every guy that comes along. Not that I'm hard-nosed or I'm gonna kick the hell out of someone. I don't want to give that impression."

Felicetta got two basic reactions. "In our opinion, he is a card-carrying bigot," said William W. Smith, a militant but widely respected black leader. ". . . The appointment of Felicetta not only reveals that concern for human relations has been stripped away by Mayor Stenvig but on the basis of present appointments can legitimately be called irresponsible."

"That's the way, Tony," Felicetta's callers said. "Sock it to 'em."

Stenvig has a thrice-broken nose (twice in football, once in boxing), and gold caps on two front teeth ("A punk kid worked me over when I tried to arrest him," he says). He wears suits off the rack, and although he is Mayor, he still talks of many things most people talk about, in the way most people talk about them. "Present from my wife," he says, pointing to large, color photos of his four children. "Just got the bill the other day, but I guess they are worth it." His own explanation of his victory agrees with those who say that the people of Minneapolis were revolting against the Establishment.

"People felt that nobody was representing them and nobody was listening," he says. "They felt alienated from the political system, and they'd had it up to their Adam's apples on just about everything. So they took a guy like me—four kids, an average home, a working man they could associate themselves with. They just said, 'Lookit, we're sick of you politicians.' "

Robert Wood is an intellectual and a political scientist. He classifies himself politically as "essentially a liberal Democrat of an organizational posture." He sees life as consisting largely of difficulties and problems. "I try to live with the difficulties," he says, "and solve the problems."

Wood was born in St. Louis in 1923 and spent most of his youth in Jacksonville, Florida. "I was brought up with traditionally Southern attitudes," he says. He served with the 76th Infantry Division during World War II, and "for a Southerner who'd been raised traditionally, the traumatic break was discovering that black troops are as good as white troops, and that dramatically changed my attitude toward the black man." After the war, he moved north, graduated from Princeton, got a master's degree in Public Administration from Harvard, and set out on a fast climb up the political science ladder. He became associate director of the Legislative Reference Bureau of the State of Florida, spent three years with the Federal Bureau of the Budget, became an assistant professor at Harvard, moved over to M.I.T., and became head of the Department of Political Science. In 1964 and 1965 he headed President Johnson's task force on urban problems, then became Assistant Secretary of Housing and Urban Development for three years and Secretary for the Administration's last month. He is now head of the Department of Political Science at M.I.T., director of the Harvard-M.I.T. Joint Center for Urban Studies (succeeding Nixon adviser Patrick Moynihan), and chairman of the board of the Massachusetts Bay Transportation Authority.

Three years ago, after the northern ghetto riots which he calls an "urban Pearl Harbor," Wood began to worry about support for the many new programs then being proposed. "I began to think one can only operate programs and reallocate resources in the U. S. by majoritarian support," he says. "So I began to worry about the long-term affect on the majority of the programs for the black and the young. Some of us began to look to see what the majority was thinking. There were no statistics, and we had to hand-craft them from the Bureau of Labor Statistics."

Wood worries about expounding on the middle American's thinking. His own opinions, he says, "go well beyond the state of present knowledge. Before we can say anything about this guy, we must differentiate the ethnic from the class. Until we get a structure of subgroups and variations, we haven't got much to go on. We don't really know their issues and their attitudes, so we really can't say very much about them. All that the press and the scholarly world have done at the present time is to identify the proposition that the majority of Americans feel dissatisfied with material prosperity, that they do not like the elite's definitions of the way the country should go, that they do not share the conviction of the special urgencies of the special minorities."

Just the same, Wood's conjectures are both provocative and precise. Politically, Wood thinks, the middle American's disposition is "Democratic in Populist terms, with some aspects of the jingoism that was the Democratic Party at the turn of the century, and with the capacity to perceive the good man and not the party. The middle American is the type of Democrat who would travel to a foreign country and return telling his friends that the roads were bumpy and the food was terrible. The upper middle class Democrat would return saying 'My goodness, the people look a little better than I thought they would.' The middle American is the little man. He is not issue-oriented, and not the type of Democrat who would turn out with the ADA. He is for the little man and access to the government, and he is suspicious of governmental power. He adheres to the bread and butter liberalism of a redistribution of resources on tax and welfare issues. He is for the FHA, but he hates welfare. He holds a basic, cultural conviction that equality of opportunity is enough. He believes that people who don't work are lazy—everybody should work. He perceives unjust distribution of resources to the undeserving and a squeeze on his part.

"Everybody is lined up and is crowded and the country is busting at the seams. The middle American says 'they' are to blame. But we all say 'they.' He does not mean the authority of the government, but essentially the 'they' of the trouble-makers, the disturbers. And that's why you get the loyalty and 'America, Love It or Leave It'—he's responding to the heavy dose of literate, critical commentary in this country in the past few years. That's why he waves the American flag—the flag represents the state of society and not the government, and it represents a bundle of things that have been pretty good to him. The middle American is the inarticulate champion of the state."

Tough Tony Imperiale, Councilman of Newark, New Jersey, has his headquarters in a one-story cinderblock building on a street of maple trees, red brick cobblestones, frame houses, and cruising ice cream wagons with their bells tinkling. There are two American flag stickers on the headquarters' front windows, an American flag is tied to a tall radio antenna on the roof, an American flag hangs on one wall inside, and a pot full of small, furled American flags sits in one corner. An oil heater squats in the front room, and its walls are decorated with pictures of Imperiale with local policemen, civic leaders, and politicians. Near the door, there is a squatting, gold-painted Buddha with a 50-calibre machine gun shell dangling around its neck. In the back is a "dojo" area, lined with plastic mats, where Imperiale practices judo and karate. On one wall, flanked by two battered foils, hangs a picture of an ancient Japanese dojo master in a Western morning coat. A string seals off the area, and a small cardboard sign hanging from it reads: "Keep out of the dojo area . . . this means you, too. Thank you. Tony."

Imperiale stands 5'6¾" and weighs 260 pounds, and he is fat and well-muscled. Ten years ago, he took over a Boy Scout troop and whipped it into "one of the sharpest troops Rubber Tree Council ever had." Three years ago, after the Newark riots, he organized a group of white vigilantes to patrol the city's North Ward and keep it quiet, and today the group has seventy-two radio cars and a red ambulance. Imperiale ran for City Council two years ago and won with by far the biggest vote of any of the twelve candidates. He admires George Wallace and the John Birch Society, and his group, the North Ward Citizens Committee, once owned an armored car. They took the armor off because of criticism, but "it doesn't take long to put that steel back on," Imperiale says. "I hope we don't have to." Now Imperiale is running for mayor, and raring to get into action against his city's hypocritical politicians, crooks, and dope pushers.

"You're looking at the next mayor of Newark," Imperiale said one afternoon late in 1969, sitting at his headquarters desk and talking to a visitor. "I intend to get rid of every quisling in that weak administration. I intend to get rid of the appeasement policy. If any militant comes in my office, puts his ass on my desk, and tells me what I have to do, I'll throw his ass off the wall and throw him off the door—black or white.

"My feet hit the deck at seven in the morning," Imperiale said. "I have breakfast with my wife and children. Then I take the children to school. I live in a poor area of town. I never moved from it. The people trust me. They come to the little city hall with their complaints. Nine times out of ten I can help them out. Our mayor doesn't want to open doors for me. But I open them doors all right. I gotta big mouth. And I got no qualms about kicking those doors right off the hinges when I have to. The only fear I do have is that they might hurt my woman and children. I'll tell you this, if they hurt my wife or children, they'll never get to court. I'll kill them with my bare hands."

"What do you say when a white liberal calls you a racist, redneck scumbag?" Imperiale was asked.

"Sometimes it gets to me," he conceded, reasonably. "But maybe I just have a rough tongue. I say to them, 'If I wasn't in the position I'm in, I'd kick the living shit out of you.' And when I take a stance, they usually back down." The stance he means is the karate stance. Imperiale learned karate after being knocked around for ten minutes by a Philippine friend in the service. "I said to myself, 'God, what is this?'" he recalls. "Every part of me hurt." He was asked if he would demonstrate his karate.

"Ralphie, come here!" Imperiale called.

A young aide named Ralph Esposito came forward, looking unhappy. Esposito drives Imperiale's $6,000 red ambulance and has a tattoo on his forearm consisting of a figure of Dennis the Menace above the legend, "Born to Break Balls." "Careful, booby," Esposito said. "Last time you did this, you busted my wrist."

Imperiale ignored him. "All right," he said cheerfully.

"Now I'm going to take Ralphie and throw him across the room."

Imperiale took Esposito over one hip and heaved him about five feet. Esposito landed hard on his back, and his eyes glazed.

"That was great!" said a photographer who was along. "Could you do it again?"

"Sure," Imperiale said. Esposito groaned, but Imperiale paid no attention, took him over his hip, and threw him about five more feet. Esposito landed on his back, and his eyes glazed again. Looking down, Imperiale discovered that he had put so much into it he had split his trousers.

So Imperiale went home to get new pants. "I'm not a stuffed shirt," he said, riding in his ambulance through the North Ward. "I go to a lot of political affairs. I went to a picnic once. The kids got me in a hot dog eating contest. I ate twenty-seven hot dogs in less than half an hour. Boy was I sick. I suffered that night. Another time I went to a German affair. Have you ever tried to tell a German you didn't want a beer? They carried me home. And I went to a Polish affair recently and ate so goddam much Kielbasa I had to have an enema. My wife called the doctor. He said, 'Give the pig an enema.'

"I got a wonderful Irish wife," Imperiale said.

The ambulance passed the corner of Mt. Prospect Street and Bloomfield Avenue and Imperiale was reminded of one evening during his campaign to clean up the city. "We came down here one night with eight guys and kicked the crap outa twenty-two junkies," Imperiale said. "Each time we came back to slap them around they lessened in ranks and finally took the hint."

"This is my castle," Imperiale said as he walked into his six-room, three-story house. In the living room there was a color TV set with a picture of Imperiale in Marine uniform on top, and the furniture was protected with clear plastic covers. There was a picture of a bullfighter on one wall, and a sawed-off shotgun stuck behind the couch. Imperiale's son was playing with a Negro friend and wanted to buy a baseball, so Imperiale gave him some change and the two boys went off to the store.

"Anyone who says I'm a bigot is a liar," Imperiale said. "We never used to fight with Negroes when I was a kid, never with Negroes. I never used the term 'nigger' until I was in the Marine Corps. I was pushed around when I was an Italian kid living in an Irish neighborhood. My wife was pushed around as an Irish kid living in a German neighborhood." He recalled that his wife's father was unhappy about acquiring an Italian son-in-law. "Every time he'd get drunk he'd say, 'Me, with a Roman in my family,' " Imperiale said good-naturedly.

Just the same, Imperiale says, "I do have a mean streak in me. If you hurt me or my wife or my children and loved ones, I'll fight." Against that possibility, he keeps a gun in every room in his house: he has about forty that are workable. He is an expert in judo and karate, and a team of associates follows him home every night. There have been two attempts on his life. One night, two Negroes shot at him outside his house, and his car was sabotaged once. His wife and children have been threatened. "Out of five thousand members we got, I can safely say that four thousand members are armed pretty well under law," Imperiale said. Besides the guns, he himself has other defenses. "This is what I love," he said, unsheathing a Bowie knife with a twelve-inch blade, and then he picked up a bayonet. "It's old, but it sticks beautifully," he said. He asked his son, back from the store, to bring him the sawed-off shotgun from behind the sofa. "This is my baby, enough to give me a good scat," Imperiale said, handling it fondly. "Want to put that behind the couch for Daddy, please?"

Imperiale put on new pants and drove back to the little city hall in his ambulance. "See that church?" he said on the way, gesturing at the enormous, stone cathedral of the Newark archdiocese. "Every stone in it was brought over from It-lee. The Bishop was supposed to live in it. But when he got here, he took one look at us Guineas and moved all the way out to Fort Lee." Imperiale laughed half the way back to the little city hall. Then he grew serious and talked about his childhood. He said he grew up poor but proud: His father earned eleven dollars a week, and his mother made soap from leftover fat. "We knew poverty, but we didn't go hungry," he said. "Our clothes had patches, but they were clean. You can be poor. But that's no reason to live like a pig. Our floors were clean. Our beds were clean. And we were clean. I'm a religious man. I'm not ashamed to say that many times I talk to God like He was right there in that seat."

7

VOTING PATTERNS—
A STEP
TO THE LEFT,
A STEP
TO THE RIGHT

*An Idea isn't responsible for
the people who believe in it.*

—DON MARQUIS

In the kaleidoscopic world of the twentieth century, a number of Americans have adopted a kind of metaphorical shorthand to help them avoid confusion. The virtue of the system is that it lets the user spot a good or bad idea by the person it comes from without having to think it through, and, conversely, to spot a good or bad person by certain catch phrases and symbols without having to listen to either him or his ideas. In this way, a liberal knows that a man with a bumper sticker reading "I Love America" is a right-winger, a super-patriot, a bigot, a Puritan, and a member of the Rotary Club, while a conservative recognizes a person with long hair as a radical, a dope-pusher, a sexual delinquent, an aider of the enemy, and a frequenter of foreign movies. Some signals mean the same to all sides: conservatives and liberals alike know that a politician who talks about law and order means to get the Negroes and lock up anybody who looks at a policeman sideways.

Using this shorthand system, some observers of middle America today have detected an impending swing to the political far right. They point to the American flag decals, the bumper stickers reading "America—Love It or Leave It," Vice President Agnew's attacks on the press and war-protestors, and President Nixon's nominations to the Supreme Court. They note that in California, the Reverend Don Moomaw, who Governor Ronald Reagan named to the Board of Education, is drawing up moral guidelines for use in the public schools; that walled communities furnishing around-the-clock protection by armed guards are doing a thriving business; and that a cutback in school funds in Los Angeles was so severe that for a long while it looked as though high school football would have to be cancelled. They point out that many bills have been introduced in state and national legislatures to clamp down on campus unrest and unleash the police during riots, and that former policemen have been elected mayors of Detroit and Minneapolis, and conclude that the armies of the right are on the move and the country is in for a period of either bloody confrontation or repression.

The trouble with the shorthand system is that it makes communication difficult and careful analysis almost impossible, and communication and analysis are important tools in understanding a technological country of 203 million people. Middle America is a region which has gone largely uncharted in the last few years, in spite of the fact that it comprises most of the U. S., and there is a scarcity of knowledge about it. Now it has been rediscovered, but the use of shorthand to describe it has some unique perils, because shorthand on a mass basis is particularly subject to error and exaggeration: the man with a flag decal on his car may be a liberal Democrat whose son got it at a gas station, Mayors Stenvig and Gribbs of Minneapolis and Detroit may or may not represent waves of conservatism, and the virulent middle Americans, like the loudest leaders of the young, may or may not have a sizeable following. One of middle America's complaints is that extremists have been allowed to take over the stage, and it would be ironic confirmation of the conviction if the extreme spokesmen for the common man were allowed to do the same.

Middle America at the start of the 1970's is a place with as many people as England and France combined and no defined borders. Beginning in 1896, when middle America deserted William Jennings Bryan and the issue of free silver to vote for William McKinley, it voted largely Republican for thirty-six years. In 1932, Franklin D. Roosevelt forged a new coalition of the poor, the Catholics, the Jews, the working men, the South, and the big city dwellers, and since then middle America has voted largely Democratic. Today, the old Roosevelt coalition is breaking up. The ethnic groups which were the backbone of liberalism have become disenchanted, the labor movement has become more conservative, and the South has been fragmented between the Democrats, the Republicans, and George Wallace's American Independent Party. Catholics, Negroes, Jews, and the poor remain largely Democratic, while Protestants, the wealthy, and those in small towns remain largely Republican.

Noting these cracks and shifts in the old voting patterns, Kevin P. Phillips, a young lawyer who was Special Assistant to Attorney General John Mitchell, last year offered a blueprint for Republican control in the 1970's in a book called *The Emerging Republican Majority*. The movement of population from the liberal cities to the more conservative suburbs and from the liberal Northeast to the more conservative South and West, Phillips wrote, gave the Republicans a chance to build a new and lasting coalition. "The upcoming cycle of American politics," he wrote, "is likely to match a dominant Republican Party based in the Heartland, South, and California against a minority Democratic Party based in the Northeast." President Nixon claims not to have read the book, and denies that his Administration is predicated on a conscious "Southern strategy," but the South clearly plays a more forceful role in his Administration than it did in that of his predecessor from Texas.

On the other side of the political fence, Democrats are working hard to re-form a coalition of their own. Former Democratic National Chairman Fred Harris has called for a "new Populism" consisting of the poor, the blacks, and the disgruntled working men. Joseph Duffey, National Chairman of the liberal Americans for Democratic Action, has urged liberals to seek out the middle Americans and learn what their problems are. "These people have legitimate reason to protest what is going on in American society," he has said, "and yet they have been neglected by liberal movements and by both political parties. For in a sense, liberalism has become an activity of the affluent, for whom the concerns of these people, like the concerns of the very poor, emerge primarily in abstract terms and categories." Representative Roman Pucinski believes that the dissastisfied, like Paul Deac's ethnic groups, are still up for grabs. "The Democratic party has as good a chance as ever," he says, "if we can come up with meaningful programs."

Whatever the strategies adopted by Republicans and Democrats, middle America will clearly be a bone of contention for at least the immediate future, because it is big, unhappy, and politically available. But politicians who wish to court middle America must first decide what sort of a mood it is in, and those who have observed middle America have come away with widely different impressions.

Some experienced observers think that there is, in fact, a resurgence of deep conservatism in middle America.

"If this situation continues," psychiatrist Bruno Bettelheim says of the alienation of the middle, "I'm very much afraid that the middle class will become radicalized on the right. It seems it will lead to a radical right and left with nothing in the middle."

"There may be a bloodbath," says Dr. Abraham Kaplan, of the University of Michigan. "Each side is saying 'Things can't go on this way,' and maybe they are right."

"The great pointed heads who know best about how to run everybody's life have had their day, and as a consequence the country's in a mess," says George Wallace. "My vote was only the tip of the iceberg. Now there's others I am responsible for: Mayor Yorty, Stenvig, both Mayoral candidates in New York [Mario Procaccino and John Marchi]. They were making Alabama speeches with a Los Angeles, Minneapolis, and New York accent. The only thing they omitted was the drawl."

"Absolute disaster lurks all around us," says former Detroit mayor Jerome P. Cavanaugh, who was once considered one of the country's brightest, young liberal mayors and decided to leave office partly because he had been tarnished with a pro-black label. "Most of our political leadership doesn't realize how desperate the situation really is, and I'm not normally a crepe hanger. The poles between the races are becoming more extreme even while more people are moving into the middle on these problems. Too often, attempts to do something provoke a reaction that does even more harm."

There is also some hard evidence that the concept of liberalism has become tainted to a great many Americans. According to a California poll in 1969, 42 per cent of all California voters thought of themselves as conservatives, an increase of 10 per cent in five years, and only 24 per cent called themselves liberals, a drop of 4 per cent in five years. In the same poll, 30 per cent of California's Democrats also called themselves conservative, an increase of 8 per cent in five years, while 31 per cent called themselves liberal, a decrease of 7 per cent in five years. In a nation-wide Gallup poll in July 1969, 24 per cent of the whites interviewed considered themselves conservative and another 29 per cent considered themselves moderately conservative, while only 14 per cent called themselves liberal and another 18 per cent said they were moderately liberal. In the same poll, 54 per cent of the whites favored the appointment of a conservative to the Supreme Court, and only 24 per cent wanted to see a liberal named.

The President and the Vice President's apparent success in wooing middle America has impressed many politicians most of all. After President Nixon's November 1969 speech on Vietnam, many war critics in Congress were convinced that he had misread the country's mood on the war and adopted a harder line than the people would tolerate. Accordingly, they made plans to hold open hearings on the war in the Senate Foreign Relations Committee. Neither the Gallup poll showing a favorable reaction to Nixon's speech nor the telegrams supporting it changed their minds, but sampling of their home districts did. The Congressmen found the mood overwhelmingly favorable to Nixon's declared policy of gradual withdrawal. After agonized and often heated debate, the plan for public hearings was scrapped.

Vice President Agnew's warm reception in much of middle America has also made a strong impression on politicians of all leanings. A liberal Republican Senator, whose views are far from Agnew's, said last year:

"We tend to forget that in the heartland of America there are millions of Americans who voted for Barry Goldwater in 1964. They are fed up with the hippie culture, they see the East Coast media as a foreign, un-American plot, they are appalled at the flesh-pots of California and Nevada, they long for the America of Edgar Guest. And to them, Agnew is a great hero. Agnew is Nixon's ambassador to the lower middle class, to the blue-collar American—the people who voted Democratic in the past, the people we used to call lunch-pail Democrats."

Yet other students of politics and middle America find little evidence of either a strong rightward swing or a revival of orthodox conservatism.

"Let's not exaggerate how reactive the white middle class is," says Nathan Glazer, professor at the Harvard Graduate School of Education and author with Daniel Patrick Moynihan of *Beyond the Melting Pot*. "Everyone has been waiting for the great swing to the right since 1964, because of the students and the Negro riots. Yet if there's been one, it's been a glacial shift. We haven't seen any vigilante action against the two groups, and we've never had the working class as quiescent and non-violent in history."

"There's not a swing to the right in this country," says Representative Allard Lowenstein, the liberal Democrat whose Long Island constituency consists mainly of middle income families. "That's nonsense. It's a swing against anarchy. They're not turning against the social reforms of the left."

"The forgotten man, that's this year's catch phrase, but I frankly don't think it's much more than that," says James Q. Wilson, professor of government at Harvard. "There's always been a very strong reaction by the middle and working classes against crime, what they take to be 'the welfare mess,' and high taxes. But it's hard to conceive of a revolution by the middle class in America, because the middle class expresses their revolution by voting for or against candidates and going to city council meetings."

"The asserted anxiety about this has been picked up by the media," Robert Wood has said, "and I wonder if it's the liberal academic and interpreter getting tired of the minority kick and looking for a new folk hero, who happens to be white."

Mesmerized by the suggestions of rampant conservatism, it is easy for liberal observers to forget that conservatism and liberalism have always struggled for supremacy in middle America and are still struggling there—often within the minds of individual voters, who disconcertingly refuse to observe the boundaries of left and right. "Populism has always had two faces in America," Paul Jacobs says. "A state like Wisconsin, for example, could produce Bob La Follette and Joe McCarthy. The same voters elected both men. The draft riots in New York City during the Civil War started out as anti-Irish, but ended up anti-black. Yet for years we believed the liberal myth that these attitudes existed only in the South."

There is considerable evidence to support this view of middle America as a place where abrupt shifts come often and sustained shifts only rarely. The victory of Senator Eugene McCarthy in the 1968 New Hampshire primary was widely read as a mandate for liberalism and peace in Vietnam. Yet polls immediately after the election suggested that most voters in New Hampshire did not even know where McCarthy stood on Vietnam, and author Richard Goodwin, a former McCarthy aide, has pointed out that McCarthy's own campaign there moved steadily away from the peace issue to the theme of change. During the last two days of his campaign, a single message was repeated every half hour on every radio station in the state: "Think how you would feel to wake up Wednesday morning to find out that Gene McCarthy had won the New Hampshire primary—to find out that New Hampshire had changed the course of American politics." In not very subtle language, McCarthy was offering the voters of a tiny state a chance to kick the Establishment in the seat of the pants. The target was different and the appeal more genteel, but the message was essentially the same as that of people in Minneapolis who urged Tony Felicetta to "Sock it to 'em, Tony"—or the message of those who, twenty-two years ago, urged their underdog President to "Give 'em hell, Harry."

Goodwin and others have noted that McCarthy even had something in common with George Wallace: they both seemed to stand outside the political system.

"This represents the same politics of participation that McCarthy talked about," Martin Stone, McCarthy's California co-chairman, has said of the unrest in middle America. "As a matter of fact, bear in mind that McCarthy himself found his greatest support in those middle class areas you're talking about. These people are appalled by violence, and sensed in McCarthy an aversion to violence. They may support one candidate who's tough and hard-nosed and promises to repress violence in the streets, and may equally support a candidate who is quiet and calm and promises peace in the streets. They don't know which way they want to go—repress violence harshly, or try to minimize it by having leaders who don't bring out violent passions. They liked Nixon because he seemed the kind not likely to bring out passions. And that's why they liked McCarthy."

The Presidential campaign of the late Senator Robert Kennedy furnished other indications of many Americans' desire for participation and their refusal to stay within convenient and conventional political boundaries. Senator Kennedy found that, second only to his call for peace in Vietnam, his call for decentralization of the government brought the greatest favorable response. After his death, a number of voters who had said they were for the Senator switched their support to George Wallace.

"They've lost faith in traditional liberalism and have a great desire for change that's non-ideological," Richard Goodwin says of the middle Americans. "Which is why you got people who voted for Bobby Kennedy in the primary voting for Wallace in the election. The lesson of 1968 was that the people who won were new faces, including Nixon, who won because of the vote against Johnson. There isn't any shift to the right. The three new Democratic Senators [Cranston of California, Eagleton of Missouri, and Hughes of Iowa] were all from the left, and the new Republican Senator [Saxbe of Ohio] seems liberal. This desire for change could easily turn into a drift to the right, but not necessarily. Stenvig could as easily have come from the left. There's a tremendous opening for new people with new approaches."

"The candidate who looks secure to him, the one who will try to get answers for him—that's the kind he'll vote for," says Mrs. Carmen Warschaw, Democratic National committeewoman from California.

"The lower class is mad, but so is the middle and the upper middle class, and I don't know why," says Kenneth O'Donnell, former special assistant to President John F. Kennedy who is running for the 1970 Democratic nomination for governor in Massachusetts. "The war is the focal point. The war is making liars of every kid under thirty— trying to find a way to beat the draft—and the parents look at them and say, 'What the hell is going on?' But what's getting them mad runs the gamut. In 1969, we held state-wide hearings on the Democratic platform. We consistently got four to five hundred people at each meeting, and ninety-five per cent of them were between thirty and forty-five years old—doctors, lawyers, professors, teachers. I'd never seen anything like it before. It used to be you'd have these things and only a handful of pols and some labor leaders would turn out.

"The public is so much smarter than when I first started in politics. Then it was no issues, just vote Democratic, vote Republican, and how to help your friends. What Gene McCarthy did was open the eyes of the people that they are the country. Before, it had been assumed that you couldn't bring a President down, that you couldn't fight the system. The McCarthy movement showed that you could."

If any despot is to appeal to middle America at the moment, in fact, he will have to be cut from a fairly socialistic mold. The *Newsweek* poll carried clear evidence that the middle Americans are not only accustomed to big government but, in some areas, want more of it. When they were asked what the government should do if it found it had collected more tax money than it anticipated, 48 per cent said the money should be used to improve conditions in the country, 34 per cent said it should reduce taxes, and 16 per cent said it should reduce the national debt. When they were asked whether the government should experiment with new ways of dealing with the nation's problems, 48 per cent said that it should and 42 per cent said that there has been too much experimentation already.

The ways in which the middle Americans wanted the government to spend its money also suggested no desire for a trimming of national domestic commitments, and considerable desire for expanding the programs in some areas. Fifty-six per cent of the middle Americans wanted more spent on job training for the unemployed. Fifty-six per cent wanted more spent on programs to combat air and water pollution. Fifty-five per cent wanted more spent to combat organized crime. Forty-seven per cent wanted more spent on Medicare for the old and the needy. Forty-six per cent wanted more spent on social security benefits. Forty-four per cent wanted more spent fighting such crimes as mugging and burglary, and 44 per cent wanted more spent to improve the nation's schools. No more than 7 per cent favored reducing any of these programs, and there was even strong support for housing programs for the Negroes whom so many middle Americans claimed already had a better chance for good housing than they did. Thirty-nine per cent wanted to see more money spent to "provide better housing for the poor, particularly in the black ghettoes," and only 13 per cent wanted such programs cut back. The middle Americans also favored increased spending for highways and public transportation, but by small margins.

The items the middle Americans wanted less money spent on stood in dramatic contrast to these areas. Without exception, they wanted programs which do not affect them directly pared down. Two-thirds of the middle Americans said that the U. S. should spend less on military aid to foreign countries, and an infinitesimal 1 per cent said the country should be spending more. Fifty-seven per cent said the country should spend less on economic foreign aid, 56 per cent said the country should reduce the amount it spends on space exploration, and only 10 per cent favored spending more

Q.   SUPPOSE THE FEDERAL GOVERNMENT IN WASHINGTON
FOUND IT HAD COLLECTED MORE MONEY IN TAXES
THAN IT HAD EXPECTED. IT COULD USE THIS MONEY TO
REDUCE THE NATIONAL DEBT, IT COULD REDUCE TAXES,
OR IT COULD USE THIS MONEY TO IMPROVE CONDITIONS
IN THIS COUNTRY. WHICH ONE OF THESE WOULD YOU
FAVOR MOST?

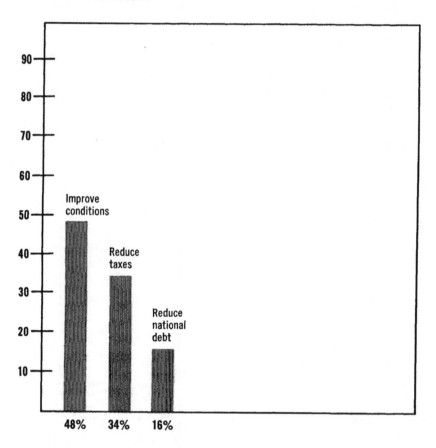

Q. SOME PEOPLE SAY THAT WE NEED TO EXPERIMENT
   WITH NEW WAYS OF DEALING WITH THE NATION'S PROB-
   LEMS. OTHERS SAY THAT THERE HAS BEEN TOO MUCH
   EXPERIMENTATION ALREADY. WHICH SIDE DO YOU
   AGREE WITH MORE?

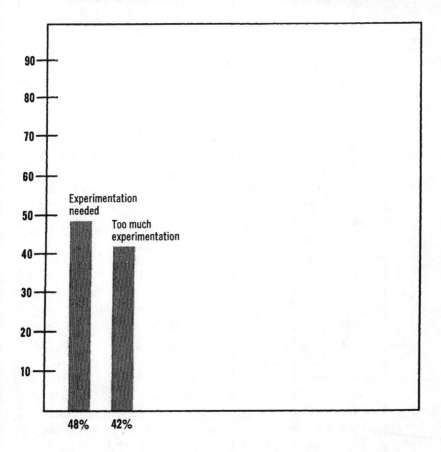

Experimentation needed — 48%

Too much experimentation — 42%

for the space program. By a margin of 26 per cent to 16 per cent, the middle Americans also said that less should be spent on military defense.

Moreover, these answers come at a time when most middle Americans think the government has been improving its performance in many domestic areas. When they were asked whether they felt the U. S. had changed for the better or the worse in certain areas, 59 per cent said it had changed for the better in providing good medical care for people like themselves and their families, while only 20 per cent said it had changed for the worse. Sixty per cent said the country had changed for the better in providing opportunities for people like themselves to get ahead, and 60 per cent said the country was doing better at providing financial security in old age for people like themselves. The one area they were dissatisfied with was housing: 54 per cent said the country was doing a worse job of providing good housing at reasonable cost for people like themselves, and only 21 per cent thought the country was doing better.

Middle America was much less sure of itself in the fields of foreign affairs and military defense, although it strongly wanted less money spent on both. The middle Americans were asked whether foreign affairs and military defense had grown so complex that they should be left in the hands of the experts in Washington, or whether people like themselves should "have something to say about them." They voted that they should have a say, but only by a margin of 50 per cent to 44 per cent. When they were asked whether the military had too much influence on foreign policy, they split into three almost equal groups: 31 per cent said the military did not have enough influence, 28 per cent said it had too much influence, and 22 per cent said its influence seemed about right.

The picture which emerges from these answers is one of deep concern about government programs close to home combined with bewilderment and impatience over programs aimed at other countries and other planets. When the middle

American says that he has been forgotten by his government, he clearly has some specific things in mind, and he wants those things taken care of: job training, pollution, crime, Medicare, social security, schools, and slum housing. It is not a list of priorities which is calculated to warm the hearts of traditional conservatives.

The *Newsweek* poll offered little comfort to orthodox liberals, either. While the liberal could see encouragement in the fact that the largest number of middle Americans would use a surplus to improve conditions, a conservative could point to the fact that 78 per cent said that their federal taxes were too high, while taxes and the high cost of living stood fourth and third on their list of national problems, and first and second on their list of local problems. The middle Americans' resentment against the Negro, his impatience with black militants and college demonstrators, his concern with crime, his distrust of the media, his readiness to give the police more power, and his willingness to let judges deny bail all loom as major obstacles to the traditional liberal way of doing things. A question on the best way to handle black demands for better education also suggested that the middle Americans favored neither traditional liberal or traditional conservative approaches to Negro demands. Although 41 per cent of the middle Americans said that Negroes had a better chance for a good education than they themselves, and only 16 per cent felt that Negroes' chances were poorer, a minuscule 3 per cent said that their demands were not justified and should be ignored. At the same time, only one-fourth said that the demands should be dealt with by moving in the direction of integrating white and black schools, and only 2 per cent favored integration by busing black children to white schools. Twenty-four per cent said that Negroes should be allowed to run and control their own schools, and 40 per cent favored improving schools where Negro children go, without saying how.

The clearest evidence of the *Newsweek* poll was that the middle American is a highly pragmatic and sometimes contradictory individual. The poll sample presumably contained both conservatives and liberals, but it was often very hard to locate them. Those who thought the Negro's chances for a job and a good education were worse than their own, for example, could be presumed to be relatively liberal, and some of their other answers supported that presumption. About 70 per cent had a favorable impression of today's young people, as opposed to 58 per cent in middle America generally, and 55 per cent felt that college demonstrators were at least partly justified, as opposed to 40 per cent in middle America generally. Two-thirds favored experimentation in dealing with the nation's problems, as opposed to 48 per cent of middle America generally, and 85 per cent said that at least some Negro demands were justified, contrasted with 70 per cent in middle America generally. Yet 69 per cent of this same group also said that half or most of the people on welfare could earn their own way if they wanted to, and more than half felt the Negro could have done something about his own slums. In the same group, 57 per cent said the police have too little power, and 66 per cent said that judges should be given the right to deny bail.

There were equivalent variations among the presumably more conservative. Of the blue collar workers who said the Negro could have improved his own slums, the largest number, 48 per cent, also would use a surplus to improve conditions, and 34 per cent favored spending more on housing for the poor, while only 16 per cent were opposed. Of those who said the Negro already had a better chance at a good job than they themselves did, 54 per cent also favored job training for the unemployed. Nor did their answers suggest that they wanted such programs for themselves. Sixty-one per cent of them said that the country had changed for the better in providing opportunities for people like themselves to get ahead.

Off-year elections traditionally provide many contradictory signs, and the elections of 1969 were no exception. Yet there had been widespread predictions of a conservative resurgence, and the resurgence did not materialize. Instead, the elections provided further evidence that the voters of America are increasingly independent and increasingly determined to show those in power, and perhaps themselves, that they still have some muscle left:

§ In Virginia, lawyer A. Linwood Holton became the first Republican governor in 84 years and his victory, together with that of William Cahill as Governor of New Jersey, was hailed by President Nixon as proof of continuing Republican resurgence. Republicans also gained eight new seats in the wealthy, urban, northern section of the state near Washington, where law and order, student radicals, high taxes, and welfare were the prime issues, and in Alexandria, John E. Kennahan became the first Republican Commonwealth's Attorney in the city's history. But Republicans picked up only one house seat outside the urban northern area, and ultra-conservative, third-party candidates fared poorly throughout the state. The *Washington Post* read Holton's victory as one of moderation over conservatism, youth over experience, and the cities and suburbs over the rural courthouses. In the Democratic primary, state senator Henry E. Howell, Jr., a populist liberal, had amazed everybody by getting enough votes to force William C. Battle, a moderate and the choice of the old Democratic organization, into a run-off. After Howell lost the run-off with 48 per cent of the vote, many civil rights leaders and labor leaders who had backed him threw their support to Holton. Holton had long been involved in the fight against segregation, and in the campaign both candidates went after the Negro vote with promises of broader black participation in government.

§ In Detroit, County Sheriff Roman S. Gribbs made crime in the streets his main issue and defeated Richard H. Austin, a Negro, by 7,000 votes out of more than half a million. During the campaign, Gribbs passed out toy police whistles stamped "Win With Gribbs," but he also avoided the catch-phrase "law and order." "Law violators must be dealt with firmly and fairly," he said. Moreover, Gribbs

had appointed Negroes to top posts in the Sheriff's department, and for a long time his opponent was given no chance
to win. White voters turned out in numbers, but many did
not make up their minds until the last minute; a poll late in
the campaign showed 18 per cent of the voters undecided,
the great majority of them white. Gribbs's narrow victory
was widely interpreted as the last gasp of white-oriented
politics in the city. Some 40 per cent of the people of Detroit
are black, and their number is growing. To win, Austin
needed better than 20 per cent of the white vote, while
Gribbs needed only 6 per cent of the black vote. Of the nine
members of the City Council elected with Gribbs, six are
liberals and three of those are black (Detroit elected its first
black councilman within the decade). Many whites who
voted for Gribbs also voted for one of the three black candidates.

One of Gribbs's first questions to reporters after winning
was about Mayor John Lindsay's showing in New York,
and he said that he is an admirer of Lindsay. "The refresh-
ing, encouraging part of my campaign," he told reporters,
"was that I encountered only warmth and encouragement
from the black voters I met. I really feel I have a rapport
with the black community."

§ In the Detroit mayoral primary, Conservative Councilwoman Mary V. Beck ran on a strong law and order
platform and promised to "sweep the streets clean of crime,
corruption, and every form of pollution." "Whether you
want to admit it or not, people are obsessed with fear," she
said. Mayor Cavanaugh "accused me of fanning the flames
of fear, but the fear is there. I go into a restaurant for a cup
of coffee, I go into the cleaners, and it's there. Can you
remember five or six years ago when you went into a drug-
store and there were no guards? I talked about the city's
fiscal situation, I talked about conservation, I talked about
urban renewal, and I could get no reaction or interest. The
issue of law and order is the big one." She finished third.

§ In Pittsburgh, where black demands for jobs had led

to counter-demonstrations by angry white union members, Democrat Peter Flaherty trounced his Republican opponent by an almost two to one margin. Pittsburgh Democrats outnumber Republicans by better than three to one, but the Republican candidate, John K. Tabor, was a Czech and was expected to have strong support among ethnic groups. Tabor said that the man who got the backlash vote "would walk off with the election," but both he and Flaherty were chary about courting such a vote openly. Tabor used television heavily and outspent Flaherty, $406,000 to $79,000. He carried only one of the city's thirty-two districts, and no ethnic voting pattern was apparent in the results. Flaherty even won handily in Italian districts where Tabor had campaigned hard on the issue of law and order. "They're more interested in taxes and community problems," Flaherty said afterward. "And they're wakened up to the realization that they're Pittsburgh voters, not racial or ethnic voters."

§ In Philadelphia, liberal Republican District Attorney Arlen Specter easily won a second term, beating a law-and-order Democrat.

§ In Boston, Mrs. Louise Day Hicks ran far ahead of the field of eighteen for nine City Council seats. A 52-year-old lady lawyer from Irish South Boston, Mrs. Hicks in 1967 had run for mayor on a platform that stressed pay raises for city employees, the forgotten man, and opposition to busing, and had almost won. "I represented the alienated voter," she said during her recent campaign, "and that's who I'm representing now, except that the number has grown." Her main issues in 1969 were high taxes, failing city services, and a government which, she said, "is concerned only about the rich and the poor." She got 76,000 votes. In second place with 47,000 votes was Thomas Atkins, a Negro graduate of the Harvard Law School who also ran on an anti-Establishment, anti-spending platform. Many of the people who voted for Mrs. Hicks voted for Atkins, too.

§ In Buffalo, New York, conservative Republican councilwoman Afreda Slominski ran on a platform of law and order and opposition to busing, expecting to pick up votes in blue-collar, traditionally Democratic districts. Representative Richard McCarthy, a Democrat, accused her of allowing herself to become the "symbol of bigotry and hate." She herself appealed to Buffalo's middle class as "the city's forgotten people." Incumbent Democrat Frank Sedita won by 20,000 votes, despite the presence in the race of a black candidate.

§ In New Jersey's gubernatorial race, a desire for change was seen as a major factor in Republican William Cahill's victory. In the Republican primary, Cahill, who refused to support Barry Goldwater in 1964, defeated a favored, law and order conservative. During the campaign, Cahill and his opponent were both moderates on the issue of law and order. Cahill told a Newark Rotary Club that drug addicts "aren't criminals. They're sick people."

§ In New York City, Republican John Marchi and Democrat Mario Procaccino got 37 per cent of the vote in the June primaries and won, and 58 per cent of the vote in the November election and lost. Incumbent liberal Republican mayor John Lindsay was reelected with strong support from wealthy whites, blacks, and Puerto Ricans and a substantial minority of the vote in many lower income white sections. Lindsay won about 32 per cent of the middle income vote, and about 27 per cent of the blue collar vote. The Jewish vote was split largely along economic lines, with wealthy Jews voting for Lindsay and middle class Jews voting for one of his conservative opponents. Procaccino spent about one-fifth of what Lindsay spent during the campaign. The night before election, he told an aide, "You can't fight City Hall." The turnout was light. "I love you all — we're the little people," Procaccino told his supporters in conceding defeat, but they wanted more potent stuff. "Law and order!" a man shouted. "Crime and corruption!" yelled a woman. "Mayor Lindsay is a fag!" a man called. "Throw him down the East River" shouted another.

§ In Atlanta, Georgia, Sam Massell, a liberal Jew, won

the pre-runoff for the mayoralty in a four-way race with a combination of black, liberal, and low income white support. A law and order candidate finished last with 18 per cent of the vote, against 31 per cent for Massell, 27 per cent for a moderate Republican, and 23 per cent for a black liberal.

§ In Seattle, Washington, a conservative, law and order Democrat finished third in the primary for mayor and didn't even make the run-off.

§ In Wisconsin, a liberal Democrat candidate for Congress won a special election against a moderate Republican who called the election "a referendum on the Nixon Administration" and implied that the Democrat had been soft on campus radicals. He was the first Democrat to win the seat in this century.

§ In Cleveland, Negro Democratic incumbent Mayor Carl Stokes narrowly defeated Republican Ralph Perk in a race which hinged on undecided whites in the $10,000 to $20,000 income bracket. On election day, more than 100 off-duty policemen, armed and in uniform, showed up at voting places in black districts to act as volunteer election challengers. Cleveland also elected a 23-year-old Councilman who had run on a law and order platform. Perk was the son of a Czech immigrant, but a local joke had it that while Stokes was black, Perk was colorless. Stokes's victory apparently ended ethnic domination of politics in the city. Three years ago, when he won by 1,679 votes, Stokes attracted 18 per cent of the white vote. In his reelection, Stokes won by 3,753 votes and got 24 per cent of the white vote.

These results offer little evidence that candidates who stray far from middle America's vast and unpredictable center will have much chance of victory in the immediate future, at least in most places. *Newsweek* polling consultant Richard M. Scammon has written that the Republican Party may well be able to build a majority for itself out of the current fragmentations of the middle, but that putting such a majority together will be tricky work.

"The problem for the Republicans is simple enough, even if the answers aren't," Scammon wrote. "For 1972 their hopes rest on the ability of the Nixon Administration to form a new coalition of the center—detaching at least some of those voters who would have been oriented to Roosevelt a generation ago and who supported Humphrey last year. Such a GOP coalition would have its own right wing (mostly in the South) and its own left (the Eastern seaboard). It would not be a sharp move to the right. A militantly conservative line might attract some of George Wallace's 9.9 million supporters from the last election. But it would alienate other voters—and ignore the many populist characteristics of the Wallace vote. Mr. Nixon is much more likely to seek a new center coalition, and if he can forge such a consenus he will win."

The strongest indication of the 1969 elections and the *Newsweek* poll is not that there is a revival of conservatism or any other orthodoxy in middle America, but that there is an expression of certain conservative values which liberal observers have forgotten in their fascination with the new forms of radicalism. The values have been there all along, and if they are now more noisily expressed, that is at least partly due to the noisy expression of the opposing radical values. Translating middle America's values into political oratory is fairly simple, but translating them into political policy is a much harder job which neither the left nor the right has apparently been able to accomplish. Basically, the middle American is demanding conservative moral values and liberal social programs, and that difficult demand is compounded by divisions within middle America itself. In one of the most basic questions in the *Newsweek* poll, the middle Americans were asked whether they favored experimentation in solving the nation's problems. The college educated, the wealthy, the young, and the white collar workers all approved experimentation by margins of almost two to one. The grade school educated, the poor, the old, and the blue collar workers all said there had been too much experi-

Q.   SOME PEOPLE SAY THAT WE NEED TO EXPERIMENT
WITH NEW WAYS OF DEALING WITH THE NATION'S PROB-
LEMS. OTHERS SAY THAT THERE HAS BEEN TOO MUCH
EXPERIMENTATION ALREADY. WHICH SIDE DO YOU
AGREE WITH MORE?

Need to experiment:

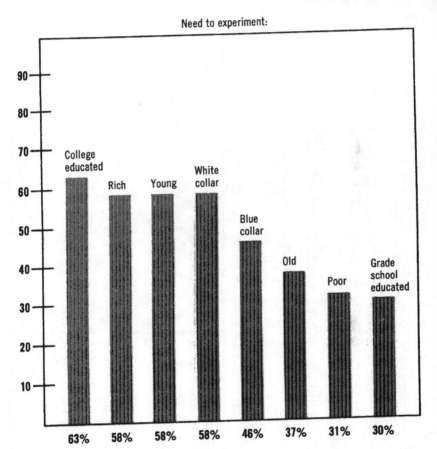

Too much experimentation:

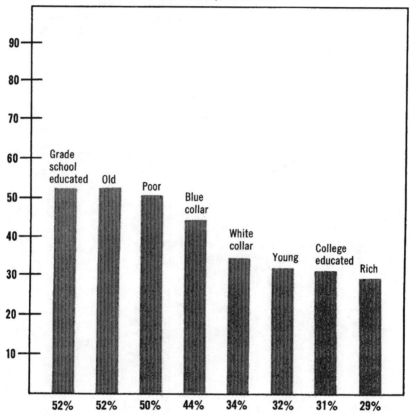

mentation, often by almost the same margins. It will not be enough for politicians to remember the middle Americans, or even to pay attention to their unifying discontents. They will have to pay attention to the varieties of the middle as well.

8

THE HIDDEN MINORITIES

The average man is the fellow who works either with his head, back, or hands.

—MARIO PROCACCINO

Americans have been brought up to think of their country as a place where many nationalities are made one through some rare and unspecified blending process. Their coins are stamped with the legend "E Pluribus Unum"—"From many, one." Their war films romanticize an Army created of Pulaskis from Cleveland, O'Haras from Chicago, Silvas from Los Angeles, and Cohens from Queens. Their orators celebrate America as a nation of immigrants, and its society has been fondly nicknamed "the melting pot." There is a lot of truth in these beliefs, but sociologists have come to believe that the melting pot is over a pretty slow flame and the blending process takes much longer than most Americans had supposed. Ethnic animosities have characterized America since the Revolution, and many of them remain. In cities,

Chinese, Italians, Irish, Germans, Scandinavians, Poles, and French tend to cluster together, suspicious of outsiders; in New York in the 1920's, it was possible to identify the residents of individual blocks not only by nationality but by region, and even by village. A recent Gallup survey reported by Father Andrew M. Greeley of the National Opinion Research Center at the University of Chicago tentatively suggested that Catholics have become more tolerant of Jews in recent years, but Jews have become somewhat less tolerant of Catholics, and the fad for Polish jokes a few years ago suggested that everybody likes to have somebody they can openly make fun of.

There are also potent sectional animosities in America. During the 1964 Presidential campaign, Republican candidate Barry Goldwater of Arizona suggested that it would be a nice thing if America could slice off the entire Eastern seaboard and float it out to sea. Northern liberals have gotten used to thinking of Southerners as red necks, Easterners see Midwesterners as hopeless rubes, and Midwesterners tend to think of both coasts as hotbeds of decadence. On top of these prejudices, there are many relatively benign differences from state to state and even city to city. The people of Minneapolis and the people of Santa Fe have little against one another, but they are as different in many ways as their ancestors from Scandinavia and Spain.

To those who still cling to the idea of America as a marvelous amalgamation of richly varied strains, these antagonisms and differences are discouraging enough—but now middle America has added itself to the list of groups with special biases and complaints. Most discouraging of all, middle America, on close inspection, turns out to have many special groups of its own. The middle Americans share many fundamental attitudes, but they are also fragmented by conflicting attitudes in at least six basic ways: ethnically, by region, by age, by income, by occupation, and most severely of all, by education.

Whether they are directed against the people of the world

outside or against each other, some of these differences between middle Americans have a vehement and even bitter
edge. Ethnic groups are often suspicious of each other and
resentful of all those of less obvious ethnic stock. "The
ethnic Americans still feel and fear that when jobs are re-
assigned, because of mechanization and all that sort of
thing," says Andrew Valuchek of the Democratic National
Committee, "that it is not going to be the Smith that is
going to lose his job, it is going to be the Pucinski." Those
in small towns are often shocked by what they see as big city
decadence. While 77 per cent of middle America and 64 per
per cent of those in medium-size cities felt that the country
had changed for the worse in its standards of morality,
among the small town pessimists who felt the country was
generally worse the figure rose to a staggering 91 per cent.

Many of the old are deeply offended by the jazzy ways of
the young. "The way they dress is outrageous," exclaimed
a 65-year-old lady in West Roxbury, Massachusetts. "They
are fresh and sassy." Many middle Americans feel victimized by the rich and the poor, but those in blue collar jobs
tend to be even more resentful of others than white collar
workers making the same amount of money. While 63 per
cent of the white collar workers said that the Negro could
have done something about his slums, 79 per cent of the
blue collar workers felt that way. The lower paid blue collar
workers in particular tend to resent what they think of as
pompous and self-righteous liberals. "There has been a def-
inite reaction on the part of our workers against liberal
candidates," says Paul Schrade, a Kennedy family friend
and a leader of the United Auto Workers. "The typical white
worker has become antagonistic toward liberals, because
the liberal preaches from his lily-white suburb while the
worker usually lives on the border line of the ghetto. He has
a large investment in his house and doesn't want anything
to happen to it. The workers are on the front lines of the
black-white conflict and resent the advice of rear-echelon
generals."

In the *Newsweek* poll, the biggest differences of all were between the middle Americans with college educations and those who never got past grade school, who were notably less confident about both themselves and society. Half of the college sample said they felt more confident about the country's ability to take care of its problems now than they had five years ago, while only one-fourth of the grade school group shared their confidence, and 52 per cent said they were less confident.

The hidden minorities within middle America are very much in agreement about many basic issues. By substantial margins, all these groups believed that the Negro had a better chance for governmental aid, that the Negro could have done something about his own slum conditions, that black militants and college demonstrators have been dealt with too leniently, that the danger of racial violence is increasing, that at least half the people on welfare could earn their own way if they wanted to, that the police don't have enough power, that judges should be able to deny bail, that the country is less religious than it was, that morality has declined, and that sex and nudity are undermining the country's morals a great deal.

But the hidden minorities also disagree about many basic subjects. They disagree on whether or not college demonstrators have some justification, on the need for governmental experimentation, on their own prospects for the future, on the purposes of an education, on whether there has been too much criticism from the young, on the importance of Vietnam and civil rights, on whether the Negro has better job opportunities than they do, on how justified Negro demands are, on the young, on their own prospects for the future, on whether the government should spend more to improve conditions, on what the government's priorities should be, and on whether the country is better or worse than it was.

On still other questions, the middle Americans split into two more or less evenly divided coalitions: the young, the almost affluent, the white collar and the college educated versus the old, the almost poor, the blue collar, and the grade school educated. The two coalitions broke up on some questions, and on others their differences were moderate, but on six issues they saw things in a markedly different light. They split on the need for experimentation, whether or not the young were too critical, their opinions of the young in general, the proper handling of college demonstrators, the usefulness of the space program, and their own prospects in the next five years.

Leonard Fein has written that "America remains, in deeply important ways, a collection of groups, and not of individuals, no matter how much liberals might wish it otherwise." Of all the groups that are collected in middle America, the one which is probably getting the most attention is the ethnic group, familiarly known to sociologists as "the ethnics."

If America's melting pot had been working the way it was advertised, the ethnic groups would by now have been dissolved in the great, All-American puree. They have not been dissolved, and they have not even been scattered throughout the mixture. In the view of many sociologists today, their most pressing problems have not even been considered or dealt with.

"There is . . . a dimension of sadness, a pathetic failure about them, an estrangement from their original vitality," Dennis Clark of Temple University has said. "The ethnic groups represent insecurity in many ways, and a great deal of nervousness about never having made it in their own country or in the United States. There is, therefore, a lot of free-flowing aggression against the neighboring groups, whoever the neighboring groups happen to be."

In the United States today there are 24 million people, or 13 per cent of the population, with at least one foreign-born parent, and another nine million people were foreign-born themselves. For many of these immigrants, immersion into American life has been an erratic process, with the new-

Q. WHAT DO YOU THINK OF YOUNG PEOPLE AND COLLEGE STUDENTS WHO ARE INVOLVED IN DEMONSTRATIONS AND SIT-INS? ARE THEY COMPLETELY JUSTIFIED IN THEIR ACTIONS, IN LARGE PART JUSTIFIED, TO SOME DEGREE, VERY LITTLE, OR NOT AT ALL?

Completely, in large part, or to some degree:

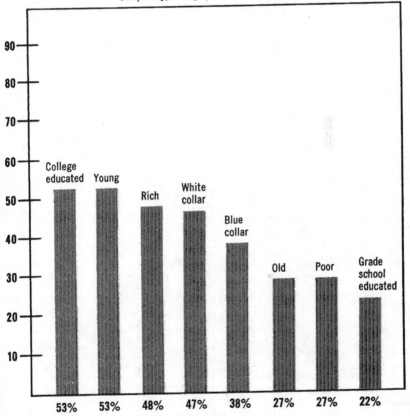

Q.   THINKING AHEAD TO FIVE YEARS FROM NOW, WOULD
     YOU SAY THINGS FOR PEOPLE LIKE YOURSELF AND YOUR
     FAMILY WILL BE BETTER, WORSE OR ABOUT THE SAME
     AS THEY ARE NOW?

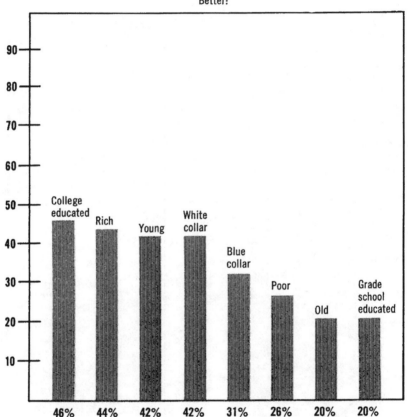

Better:

College educated	Rich	Young	White collar	Blue collar	Poor	Old	Grade school educated
46%	44%	42%	42%	31%	26%	20%	20%

Q. COMPARED WITH FIVE YEARS AGO, DO YOU FEEL MORE
CONFIDENT OR LESS CONFIDENT ABOUT THE ABILITY
OF THIS COUNTRY TO SOLVE ITS PROBLEMS?

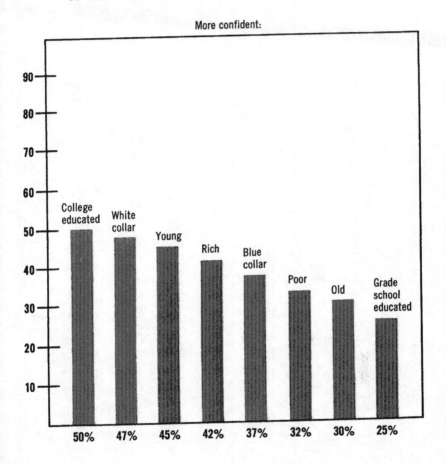

Q. COMPARING THIS COUNTRY WITH WHAT IT WAS LIKE TEN YEARS AGO, DO YOU THINK THIS COUNTRY HAS CHANGED FOR THE BETTER OR FOR THE WORSE?

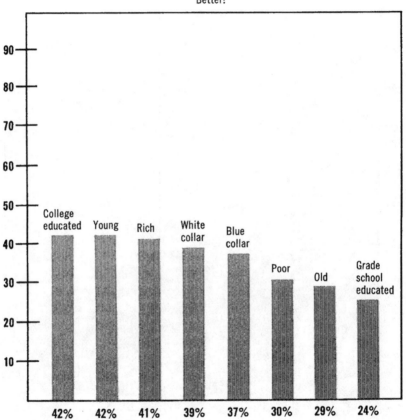

Better:

College educated	Young	Rich	White collar	Blue collar	Poor	Old	Grade school educated
42%	42%	41%	39%	37%	30%	29%	24%

Q. IN YOUR OPINION, DO NEGROES TODAY HAVE A BETTER CHANCE OR A WORSE CHANCE THAN PEOPLE LIKE YOURSELF TO GET A GOOD EDUCATION FOR THEIR CHILDREN?

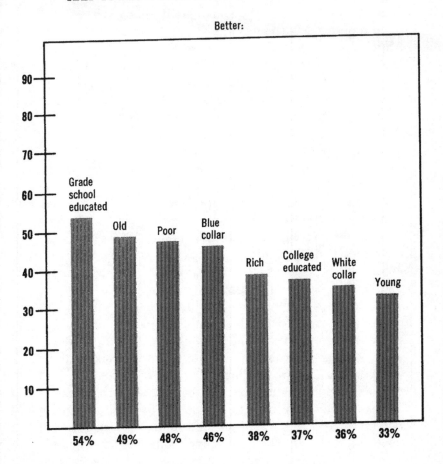

Better:

Grade school educated	Old	Poor	Blue collar	Rich	College educated	White collar	Young
54%	49%	48%	46%	38%	37%	36%	33%

comer shedding certain old attitudes and picking up new ones. Psychologists have observed that people traveling in even the least strange of foreign countries tend to feel a bit uneasy, and it is a sign of the immigrant's uneasiness that he often requires new feelings of loyalty for the country he left behind. The first Lithuanian newspaper was not published in Lithuania, but in New York City. The nation of Czechoslovakia, Nathan Glazer has written, was actually launched at a meeting in Pittsburgh. During World War II, most southern Italians were indifferent to their country's war with Ethiopia, but many southern Italians in America became staunch supporters of it. The ethnic groups in America are therefore not only different from each other, they are different from their relatives back home.

Collectively, the ethnic groups form a majority in many large American cities. In 1960, 19 per cent of all New Yorkers were foreign-born whites, another 28 per cent were the children of foreign-born whites, 14 per cent were Negroes, and 8 per cent were Puerto Ricans. Of the remaining 31 per cent, many were only two or three generations removed from a foreign country and were closely tied to ethnic customs through their families, leaving only about one in five New Yorkers as WASPs who looked on themselves as native stock. But the various members of these ethnic majorities are in different stages of a complex and constantly changing process. On the one hand, they are being assimilated into their new land: by the second generation, most of them have abandoned their parents' native language. On the other hand, they still bear their ethnic identities and are different from others—including those in other ethnic groups—in their new country. They often retain identifiable ethnic characteristics. The Irish tend to bear pain stoically, worry little, enjoy life, and be the most liberal. The Italians worry a lot and enjoy life a lot, too, and they score fairly high on tests of prejudice. The Irish are the most apt to become alcoholics of any ethnic group. The

Jews rarely become addicted to alcohol but have the greatest susceptibility to drug addiction.

While the ethnic group as a whole is slowly becoming assimilated into American society, the composition of the group itself changes. "Parts of the group are cut off, other elements join the group as allies," Nathan Glazer and Daniel Patrick Moynihan wrote in *Beyond the Melting Pot*. The children of an Italian woman and an Irish man will be regarded as Irish, while the children of an Irish woman and a Jewish man will be regarded as Jews. At the same time, the function of the ethnic group is often changing. The ethnic groups often become interest groups by dominating various businesses and professions. Jews dominate the jewelry and garment business, Irishmen tend to become lawyers, politicians, or policemen, and many Germans go into engineering. Columnist Joseph Kraft has noted that Mayor John Lindsay of New York ran afoul of several of these ethnic-professional groups and, in the course of trying to solve certain city problems, lost considerable popularity with the ethnic groups concerned. Lindsay attacked the city's old bureaucracies with reformist zeal, but, to those who had relied on the bureaucracies for jobs, he seemed to be attacking them personally, and they fought back. The Irish police beat him on the issue of a Police Review Board. The Jewish teachers fought him to a draw over decentralization in Ocean Hill-Brownsville, and the sanitation men, composed of various ethnic groups, threw the city into near-paralysis by walking out.

These chosen professions, in turn, affect the ethnic groups' relations with each other. Jewish apartment house owners may dislike anti-discrimination laws which limit their freedom to operate, but they will be inhibited from protesting too loudly by the general Jewish commitment to laws aimed at discrimination. Italian, Irish, and German homeowners, however, have often competed directly with Negroes for jobs, and their economic fears for their property are reinforced by their view of the black man as a competitor.

In America, many of the ethnic groups have traditionally regarded each other with suspicion and hostility, and their attitude toward Negroes today may be no more or less racist than their attitudes toward other nationalities in the past. Father Andrew M. Greeley of the University of Chicago has written that he knows of no accusation against the black man—including the charges that he is lazy, shiftless, irresponsible, pleasure-loving, immoral, and culturally inferior—which were not also made against the Irish in America. The major difference between the emerging black man and the emerging Irishman so far, Greeley pointed out, is that the Irish were more violent. Thirty-four people died in the Watts riots of 1965, but hundreds died in the anti-draft riots of 1863, and the Irish Molly McGuires engaged in extensive guerilla warfare, which no black group in America has yet done.

The inter-ethnic animosities are muted today, but they are still very much alive. An Irish priest is seldom welcome in a Polish parish, or vice versa. Invasion of one ethnic neighborhood by another ethnic group has always constituted a powerful threat to the emotional security of the older group. "When I was growing up on the west side of Chicago," Greeley has written, "an Italian family was only a little more welcome in an Irish neighborhood on the south side than a Negro family would have been." The threat posed by such newcomers is quite real. The infusion of a new ethnic group threatens to disrupt all the older group's familiar ways of life, including their friendships, their stores, their churches, and their day-to-day social lives.

But while ethnic groups may retain their identities for many generations, their relations with the outside world steadily evolve. Greeley has tentatively identified the stages of this evolution as isolation, organization and self-consciousness, militancy, embarrassment at recent militancy, and, finally, adjustment. Toward the end of this evolution, the emerging ethnic group may try to prove its assimilation by showing that it is more American than anybody else; Moynihan has said that the McCarthy era gave the Irish at Fordham a welcome chance to prove that they were more patriotic than the WASPs at Harvard. The notion of Uncle Tom, Greeley believes, is common to all ethnic groups, which do not take kindly to outside suggestions about who their leaders should be and tend to suspect any member of the group who is on blatantly good terms with outsiders.

The ethnic group's stage in the evolutionary process may also be a strong factor in its relations with other ethnic groups. Greeley believes that the currently strong animosity of Poles to Negroes is not a reflection of any cultural prejudice but of assimilation. The Polish are relatively recent arrivals in America, and they are understandably alarmed about the value of their hard-won property. Education affects many of these attitudes, and the Polish antagonism to Negroes is not as great among those with college educations, but education is not a perfect leveler. In one survey, 51 per cent of the Irish Catholics in college agreed with the Kerner Commission's basic finding that "White racism is the cause of Negro riots in the city," but only 34 per cent of German Catholics in college agreed with the statement. Similarly, 37 per cent of Scandinavian Protestants in college agreed with the Commission, and only 28 per cent of their German Protestant counterparts. Moreover, time alone may not melt away all ethnic differences, and events can sometimes slow or turn back the assimilation process. "The rise of Negro militancy," Representative Pucinski says, "has brought a revival of ethnic orientation in all the other groups."

Ethnic identity is both a shield and a barrier for immigrant groups, and professionally, it can provide both an opportunity and a trap. A doctor, a politician, or a contractor may achieve much greater success with his own ethnic clientele than he would be able to achieve outside it, but the outside world often fails to honor his achievement.

A man who rises swiftly within a Catholic college often finds it difficult to keep rising by moving to a non-Catholic school. Yet the ethnic institutions and social units offer a kind of security to immigrants, and today many of these units are being disrupted. Less than a generation ago, the labor union, the political club, the neighborhood and the church all served as buffers between the immigrant and the large, strange, and complex society beyond. Today, the unions and the churches have often grown large and impersonal. The leaders of the churches often seem to be taking sides with the threatening outsiders, the Negroes, while the local political clubs have all but disappeared. In many cities, large, cold housing projects have replaced entire neighborhoods, and the friendly stores, churches, and social clubs are nowhere to be seen.

The ethnic groups are not consistently liberal or consistently conservative politically, although they were an important part of Franklin D. Roosevelt's winning coalition, but socially they tend to be old-fashioned. They may or may not be more alienated than other middle Americans today, but they are probably less secure and the various turmoils of the sixties probably upset them even more. They believe in their new country, and they feel that the free enterprise system has worked for them. They set a high value on work, and they look down on welfare recipients. They themselves often refuse to apply for poverty programs even when they know they are eligible. They particularly resent the demands of some Negroes for reparations for past injustices, because they believe in America as a country which offers no preferential treatment to anybody.

Today, many members of these ethnic groups feel that they have been forgotten, and they are puzzled. They see what they consider favoritism toward the Negro, and they are resentful. They see the Negro making inroads on their neighborhoods, and they are alarmed. When they express their resentment and alarm they feel they are accused of bigotry, and they are angry.

"They see no programs directed at them or their kids," Irving Levine of the American Jewish Committee has said, "they see their taxes rising and neighborhood services getting worse, they see the intelligentsia on television depict them as bigots and backlashers and they're furious and can only shout: 'All right, I'm a bigot if that's what you want.' "

"The very fact that the ethnics have become acculturated, though not assimilated," Father Andrew Greeley has written, "will make them more, rather than less, difficult to work with."

Because they are both diverse and constantly changing, and because they have been ignored by scholars until recently, the ethnic groups probably present the greatest challenge of any group within middle America. Even today, there is scanty scientific interest in them. Father Greeley has reported that the last serious sociological study of American Poles was done in 1918. "Ethnic questions are not routinely included in survey questionnaires," he has written, "and for all the wild assertions about ethnic voting patterns (based usually on the foreign-born percentages of the Census tract data), national samples of political behavior rarely break down the American religious groups into their various ethnic components. . . . Yet, anyone who argues that ethnic research is important is told first that the question is quite irrelevant because of the workings of the assimilation process, and second that it is a highly sensitive issue which might offend people if pushed too vigorously. How something can be irrelevant and sensitive, no longer an issue and still offensive, is one of the great paradoxes that we gentlemen adventurer sociologists must learn to live with."

No such qualms stand in the way of those who would study the old and the young or the rich and the poor in America, but the celebrated gaps between these various groups are sometimes wider and sometimes narrower than most Americans have come to believe. In a study by social psychologist Dr. Vern Bengston of 500 college students in

California, 80 per cent of the sample reported that communication between themselves and their parents was good, and Samuel Lubell has reported that only about 10 per cent of college students he had studied have serious difficulties with their parents. In the *Newsweek* poll, income alone was usually less of a factor in the middle American's thinking than the way in which he earned his living.

Both the rich and the poor stand outside middle America, but they were included in the larger sampling which The Gallup Organization made for *Newsweek,* and the differences between income groups are best illustrated by comparing their answers. On virtually all questions where income made a difference in the answers, the wealthy stood at one pole, the poor at another, and the middle Americans in between. On certain questions, the differences between these income groups was great.

George Wallace has been presumed to draw much of his support from the lower economic groups, and the poll confirmed the presumption. In the national sample, 84 per cent of those earning more than $15,000 a year thought the country would be in poorer shape with Wallace as President, but only 57 per cent of those earning less than $5,000 a year agreed; in middle America, 68 per cent felt that things would be worse under Wallace. The poor were notably less tolerant of college demonstrations: 43 per cent said they were completely unjustified, as opposed to 29 per cent of the wealthy. Contemplating young people in general, 73 per cent of the wealthy and only 42 per cent of the poor felt favorably disposed. The wealthy were notably bolder: 58 per cent of them favored experimentation in solving the nation's p.oblems, and only 31 per cent of the poor welcomed further experimentation. As might be expected, the wealthy had a more cheerful view of their own circumstances, but even they were far from satisfied. Forty-six per cent of the wealthy and 24 per cent of the poor said they were better off than they had been five years ago, while 44 per cent of the wealthy and 26 per cent of the poor ex-

Q.   IS YOUR OPINION OF YOUNG PEOPLE TODAY FAVORABLE
     OR UNFAVORABLE?

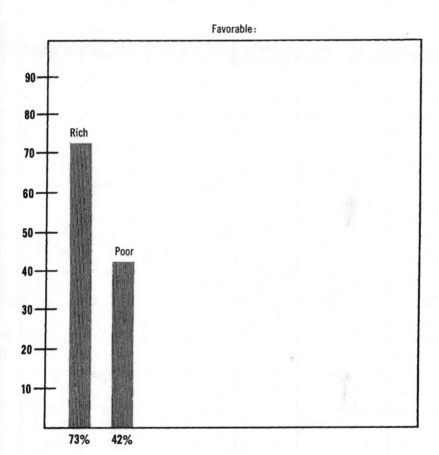

Favorable:

pected to be better off in five years. Comparing the country in general with what it was like a decade ago, 41 per cent of the wealthy said it was now better and 42 per cent said it was worse, while 30 per cent of the poor said it was better, and half of them said it was worse.

The poor were notably more hostile toward the Negro, the media, and their government than the wealthy, and they had considerably less sympathy with changing moral standards. Seventy-nine per cent of the wealthy and 55 per cent of the poor found at least some Negro demands justified. Sixty-two per cent of the wealthy and 74 per cent of the poor felt that the Negro could have done something about his slum conditions, although the response of the poor was almost exactly that of the middle Americans. Three-fourths of the wealthy and 58 per cent of the poor put some faith in the truthfulness of the media and the government, while 72 per cent of the poor and 58 per cent of the wealthy believed that sex and nudity were undermining the nation's morals a great deal. The poor were not notably angrier about high federal taxes, but they were notably more critical of the local taxes they had to pay.

Income alone also produced some splits within middle America. Civil rights was listed as a major national problem by 40 per cent of the upper middle income group and by only 33 per cent of the lower middle income group. The lower middle income group was somewhat more inclined to say that crime and drug use by young people in their community was "very serious," that more money should be spent on social security benefits, that less should be spent on space programs. Somewhat surprisingly, they were more inclined to say that the U. S. is too materialistic, and that they should have a say in foreign and military policies. But on most questions, the differences based on income alone were far smaller than the differences based on occupation and education.

Within middle America, the young were more confident but not always more liberal than their elders. The *News-*

Q. HOW MUCH DO YOU THINK THAT NEWSPAPERS, MAGA-
ZINES, RADIO AND TELEVISION CAN BE TRUSTED TO
TELL THE TRUTH ABOUT WHAT IS GOING ON IN THE
WORLD TODAY—CAN THEY BE TRUSTED A GREAT DEAL,
SOME, LITTLE, OR NOT AT ALL?

A great deal or some:

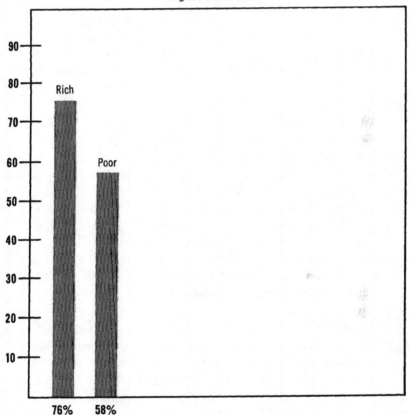

week sample was broken down into three categories by age: those under 30, those 30 to 55, and those over 55. Compared to the older group, twice as many of those under 30 felt that things had gotten better for them in the past five years, and twice as many expected things to be better five years from now; the old tended to think that things had stayed about the same and would change little in the future. Forty-two per cent of the young and only 29 per cent of the old felt that the country had changed for the better in the past decade. The young were less inclined to feel that society was favoring Negroes at their expense: 37 per cent of the young and half of the old said that the Negro's job opportunities were better than theirs.

The young were also markedly bolder in their thinking about the country: 58 per cent of the young and 37 per cent of the old said that experimentation was needed; 64 per cent of the young and 49 per cent of the old said that criticism was needed; and 58 per cent of the young and only 35 per cent of the old favored using a government surplus to improve conditions in the country. Their priorities were also different. The young favored more money for schools (which they rated more poorly than their elders did), pollution, and crime. The old favored spending more on crime, social security, Medicare, and transportation. When they were asked what the goal of a young person today should be, almost two-thirds of the young said that he should do anything he wants to, regardless of money, while 57 per cent of the old said that he should get an education that would train him for a good job. The old were far more critical of the space program: 71 per cent said that less should be spent on space, while only 46 per cent of the young would cut the space budget. The young were far more confident about their own grasp of governmental complexities: 61 per cent of the young and only 40 per cent of the old believed that they should have a say in foreign and military affairs.

On the other questions, the different attitudes of the dif-

Q. COMPARING THIS COUNTRY WITH WHAT IT WAS LIKE TEN YEARS AGO, DO YOU THINK THIS COUNTRY HAS CHANGED FOR THE BETTER OR FOR THE WORSE?

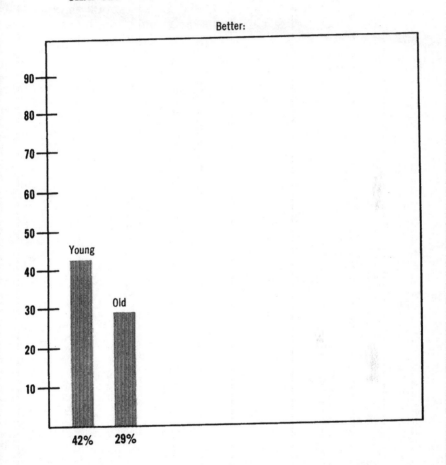

Better:

Q. SUPPOSE THE FEDERAL GOVERNMENT IN WASHINGTON
    FOUND IT HAD COLLECTED MORE MONEY IN TAXES
    THAN IT HAD EXPECTED. IT COULD USE THIS MONEY TO
    REDUCE THE NATIONAL DEBT, IT COULD REDUCE TAXES,
    OR IT COULD USE THE MONEY TO IMPROVE CONDITIONS
    IN THIS COUNTRY. WHICH ONE OF THESE WOULD YOU
    FAVOR MOST?

Improve conditions:

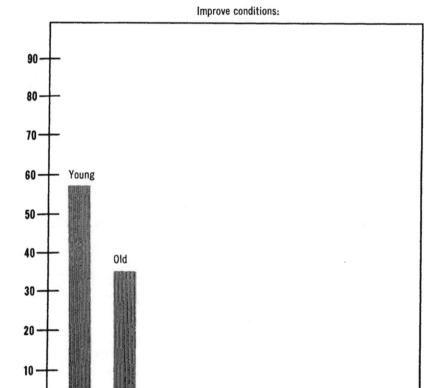

58%   35%

ferent age groups were more surprising. The old predictably took the dimmest view of today's young, but the young themselves were less sympathetic than those 30 to 55: 47 per cent of the old, 58 per cent of the young, and 64 per cent of the middle aged said they had a favorable opinion of most young people today. Seventy per cent of the old said that college demonstrators had little or no justification, and although the young were more tolerant, 46 per cent of them said that the demonstrators had little or no justification. The young were very slightly more inclined to say that federal taxes were too high, and they were somewhat less inclined to say that the U. S. troops should never have gone into Vietnam. They were a great deal more inclined to say that people were less religious than they used to be: 62 per cent of the old and 81 per cent of the young felt that way. And although fewer of the young than the old felt that the country's morality had changed for the worse, 72 per cent of the young agreed that it had, and half of them said that sex and nudity were undermining morality a great deal.

The differences in outlook between blue collar workers and white collar workers in middle America were far more basic and surprising than the differences of either age or income alone. In the *Newsweek* poll, the blue collar workers were consistently less confident about their country, less confiident about their own prospects for the future, less inclined to say that their life was improving, angrier at today's young, angrier at militants and demonstrators, more resentful of the Negro, and angrier about taxes and the high cost of living than white collar workers in the same income brackets. On many of these questions, the differences between the blue and white collar outlook was dramatic:

§ Among blue collar workers, 42 per cent were less confident about their country's ability to handle its problems than they had been five years ago, and 37 per cent were more confident. Among their white collar counterparts, 47 per cent were more confident, and 36 per cent were less confident.

§ In the lower middle income group especially, blue collar workers were notably less inclined to say that they felt better off and to expect that they would be better off five years from now: 44 per cent of the white collar workers and 34 per cent of the blue collar workers said they were better off now than they had been, while 42 per cent of the white collar workers and 31 per cent of the blue collar workers expected to be better off in the near future.

§ On a question asking whether the Negro's chances for good housing were better, worse, or equal to their own, the largest number of white collar workers, 38 per cent, said that they were worse, while the smallest number of blue collar workers, 25 per cent, said that they were worse.

§ When they were asked whether the Negro could have done anything about his own slum conditions, 63 per cent of the white collar workers and 73 per cent of the blue collar workers said that he could have. Thirty-eight per cent of the white collar workers and 49 per cent of the blue collar workers felt that the Negro's job opportunities were better than their own.

§ When they were asked whether the country would be better off or worse off if George Wallace were President, 63 per cent of the blue collar workers and 75 per cent of the white collar workers said it would be worse off.

§ When they were asked the proper goal for today's youth, 52 per cent of the blue collar workers said they should get an education for a well-paying job, and 59 per cent of the white collar workers said they should do whatever they wanted to do, regardless of money.

§ Seventy-three per cent of the white collar workers and 82 per cent of the blue collar workers said their federal taxes were too high, and the blue collar workers earning $10,000 to $15,000 were the maddest of all: 88 per cent of them said their federal taxes were too high, compared to 68 per cent of their white collar counterparts.

Q. THINKING AHEAD TO FIVE YEARS FROM NOW, WOULD
   YOU SAY THINGS FOR PEOPLE LIKE YOURSELF AND YOUR
   FAMILY WILL BE BETTER, WORSE, OR ABOUT THE SAME
   AS THEY ARE NOW?

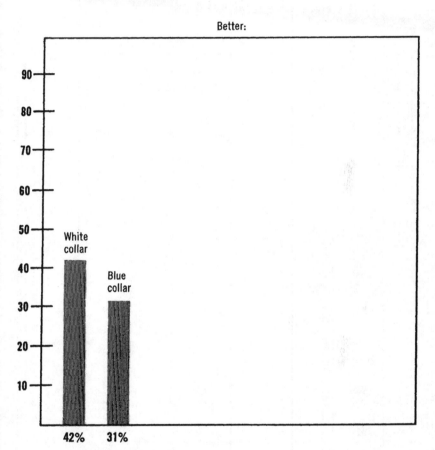

Better:

White collar 42%   Blue collar 31%

Q. WHAT DO YOU THINK IS MORE IMPORTANT FOR A YOUNG PERSON TO DO TODAY—GET AN EDUCATION THAT TRAINS HIM FOR A JOB THAT PAYS WELL, OR DO WHAT HE REALLY WANTS TO DO EVEN IF IT MEANS HE WILL NEVER MAKE MUCH MONEY?

Do what he wants to do:

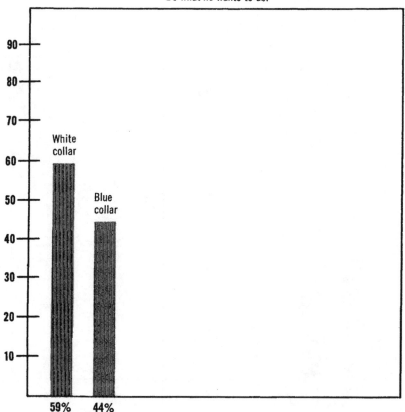

59%   44%

§ When they were asked whether they viewed today's young favorably or unfavorably, 54 per cent of the blue collar workers and 66 per cent of the white collar workers said their opinion was favorable.

The blue collar worker emerges from these answers as a much less secure and much less tolerant individual than his white collar counterpart, and many experts believe that the explanation lies both in the nature and relative insecurity of his job. In his Bemis Lecture, Robert Wood noted that for both the blue and white collar worker "the frontiers of his career expectations have been fixed since he reached the age of thirty-five, when he found that he had too many obligations, too much family, and too few skills to match opportunities with aspirations," and the assessment is even more applicable to the blue than the white collar man. Wood also noted that it is the working man who most typically refuses to make room in his plant, his schools, and his neighborhood for Negroes and other unemployed minorities.

"As we bring blacks and other minorities, as we must, into industry and jobs," says Mitchell Sviridoff of the Ford Foundation, "we perhaps should be concerned about the guy already working in a low-skilled or semi-skilled job. We should be concerned about a serious investment in upgrading his education and skills. This would benefit both the minorities and the white workers in opening up new jobs and improving opportunities for advancement. This would mean radical new things, like bringing education into the shops and plants, or the development of a radical new co-operative education where a worker would spend, say, three months working and three months going to school with substantial scholarship support."

Both blue and white collar workers suffer the same estrangement from America's current culture that the middle American in general suffers. "His plight, his point of view he never sees when he puts on that damned TV," says Gus Tyler of the International Ladies' Garment Workers Union. "The beautiful people are there, the intellectual wise guys are there, and the blacks are there. He's not there. And when he is, he comes through as pretty much of a jerk, run by a nagging wife. And that's not the proletarian view at all."

But for the blue collar worker, as for the ethnic groups which make up a large part of the blue collar force, these omissions and distortions are particularly important. The blue collar worker has less security in his job, even though some are making as much as the white collar worker. As the *Newsweek* poll indicates, he is also less secure about himself and more suspicious of the world outside. Both his experience and his horizons tend to be narrower than the white collar worker's. He has a strong need to feel that he has a place in society.

Within the working class, moreover, the young have some special problems of their own.

Lewis Carliner, professor of labor studies at Rutgers, has written that the young worker is under more serious economic pressure than his elders, yet is forced to pay for many programs that benefit his elders only. The young worker is often in debt, because he has a wife and young children to support and house furnishings to buy. His mortgage rate is higher than his elders', and inflation squeezes him more because he must buy more items. His assets are a fraction of the older blue collar workers'. In 1963, workers under 35 had total assets of $6,304, while those 35 to 44 had assets of $16,008, and those 55 to 64 had assets of $32,527— including about $12,000 in investments.

As these figures indicate, the blue collar worker's economic status improves dramatically when he moves into middle age. His children become independent and then self-supporting, and his wife often gets a job. His installments have largely been paid off. His cost of living drops appreciably when his children move out, and when he reaches retirement age he begins collecting the benefits which the hard-pressed young worker is helping to pay for.

The young blue collar worker, therefore, shares some of the resentments toward the older generation which many college students feel. But the young member of the working class is not a rebel. By and large, his goal is to earn a little more than his father did, and to live simply and securely. He resists change, and the black man often becomes a symbol of change and disturbance to him. Yet the institutions of society have apparently sided with this enemy, and the young blue collar worker is apt to be particularly resentful toward what seems the cruelest blow of all: the actions of Catholic priests who take up the Negro's cause.

In a paper published last year, three sociologists, William Simon, John Gagnon, and Donald Carns, drew a picture of the young blue collar worker as a man at sharp odds with much of what is happening around him. According to the sociologists, the young worker is "conservative and wedded to traditional values." He has no use for drugs, and he does not want to throw out the ways of the older generation. He is ready to take life as it comes "as long as it comes in predictable ways." He likes to work with things, not people, and attempts to make his work more rewarding often only upset him. Yet he sees turncoats all around him. Many young people, including many members of the middle class, wear mod clothes, and that upsets him more than the queer ways of the hippies, whom he can dismiss as irrelevant to him.

The forces of change even infiltrate his own house. His wife is much more inclined to try the new styles than he is, and she is much more eager for an active social life. He wants his home only to be a quiet refuge where he can relax. He sets great store by manliness, which to him means keeping your thoughts to yourself and your emotions in check. When things go in ways that he does not like, as they often do today, he does not explain them with the psychological jargon that many members of the upper class and upper middle class use. He falls back on the only language he knows, the moral language he was raised on. In today's unsettling society, he is increasingly apt to define the issues in moral terms.

The young worker is not a part of any youth movement,

188 / THE TROUBLED AMERICAN

and he is not a part of the "now generation." He is a part of
the "then" generation, and unless he changes, which is the
last thing he wants, he is likely to represent a conservative
force in the country for years to come. Since 1960, the number of people under 25 in the work force has increased from
13 million to about 20 million, while the number of workers
over 45 has increased only 18 per cent and the number between 35 and 44 has actually declined. Today, nearly half
of all union members are under 40, and in the near future,
labor leaders will have a constituency which is either old or
young, with the young in the majority.

The social conservatism of the blue collar worker, therefore, is going to be a force in American society for many years,
yet today it is probably under greater attack than ever before
in history. It is threatened at the blue collar worker's job, in
his neighborhood, in his home, and on the TV set that keeps
him in daily touch with the larger world, and society itself
does not seem to care whether his values survive or not.

"Look," says Nicholas Kisburg of the Teamsters Union,
"this guy has a large commitment to the work ethic and
he feels threatened and sees people making fun of the work
ethic and he's confused and angry as hell. He's the s.o.b.
who could really burn the country down."

Delegates to the 1969 convention of the United Auto
Workers, who are among the best paid workers in the country, carried signs reading "Dignity Now." Many middle
Americans support that demand, and they are adding a
demand for simple recognition from other segments of
American society, from whom they have become increasingly isolated. So far, the demands have not been met.

"Many of the young people see this group as made up of
large-bosomed, beer-drinking, drum and bugle corps types,"
says Representative Allard Lowenstein. "It strikes them as
artificial and comical."

"A large reason for the growing alienation of the white
working class is their belief that they are not respected,"
columnist Pete Hamill wrote in *New York Magazine* last

year. "It is an important thing for the son of an immigrant to be respected."

"They feel looked down upon because their manners are untaught," writes Michael Novak, a sociologist at the State University of New York, "and then they witness the sons and daughters of the privileged violating with impunity every inhibition they themselves have been forced to nurture."

"This group, without being able to state it or perhaps even knowing it fully, is dissatisfied with the elitist contempt for the working people," says Nat Goldfinger, economist for the AFL-CIO. "The Wallace campaign tended to bear this out."

"The only thing the white middle class needs is an occasional pat on the back for a job well-done," says Bruno Bettelheim. "Not this constant abuse, but a little praise. If they were given credit for what they've done in their life, this country would be much better off, but no, always something bad. These people aren't bad, they're only human, and the people who criticize them have no right."

9

THE
EDUCATION GAP

In American society today, there is a sharp cleavage between the wealthy, the intellectuals, and the liberals, on one hand, and most of middle America, on the other, and a surprising amount of the separation is traceable to education. In the *Newsweek* poll, the most dissatisfied middle Americans were those with only grade school educations, the most satisfied were those who had been to college, and the widest divergence in attitude was the one between these two groups. The gap between the grade school educated and those outside middle America is so much greater that a small but rapidly growing number of educated leaders look down their noses at the under educated who, until very recently, constituted the majority of American society. Unlike other American problems, the education problem is certain to diminish, not grow. But until it does, America runs the risk of creating a split society in which the educational haves and have nots regard each other with disdain and fury across a steadily widening gulf.

The educated American's disdain for middle class chauvinism has a long and often honorable history. It goes back at least to Sinclair Lewis' *Babbitt,* a fierce attack on mind-less boosterism in the middle class, where slogans replaced thought, and getting ahead and being well-liked were the twin goals of every right-thinking man. During the forty-eight years since that book was written, however, the disdain has broadened and taken on a nasty tinge, until today many of the well-educated sneer at the trappings of middle America without troubling to learn what the trappings represent. In the process, this new elite has grown steadily farther away from the life of a large segment of the population for whom normality is a virtue. "They don't like non-normal behavior," Representative Edward Derwinski of Chicago says of the ethnic groups in his district.

Today, a number of people who qualify for membership in the intellectual elite are saying that it is time to call off the condescension. One of the most prominent is the 64-year-old Japanese president of San Francisco State College who, with one yank on the cord of a demonstrating student's bull horn, transformed himself into a minor hero to all those who have had enough.

Dr. S. I. Hayakawa is a small, quick, nervous professor of language who two years ago was elevated to the presi-dency of San Francisco State. "I've been, all my life, the kind of intellectual highbrow I disapprove of," he says. But today he is deeply concerned about the educational gap in the United States.

"This great middle class majority didn't just spring up," Hayakawa said recently, pacing rapidly up and down his office and stopping occasionally to perch on the edge of his desk. "They've been there all along, but the college-educated classes have been moving farther and farther away from the middle and lower middle classes. Their professors teach them to look down on the American Legion, Lions Club, and the Rotary—all the popular manifestations of everyday culture. The professors represent a value system that is for-eign to the middle class.

"We have an educational system that alienates people

from middle America. The problem is how to produce an educated class that stays in touch with middle America, and I don't know how we can do that. The duty of the liberal intellectual today is to keep middle America from turning to right-wing cops as the only answer. He's got to show some sympathy for the mother whose son is killed in Vietnam, and not give it all to the kid who burns his draft card. He's got to take a stand against obscenity, instead of saying it's all very cultural and chic and aren't you square for not going along. The intellectual has to acknowledge his common humanity with the shoe clerk, the accountant, and the freight handler."

So far, the educational split in America has scarcely been noticed, much less studied. But it is unmistakably there. A 1969 poll by Daniel Yankelovich suggested that the college and non-college classes look at life differently, define their goals and enemies differently, and act differently. (In the poll, some 70 per cent of the college group and only 30 per cent of the non-college group had taken part in some form of protest.) Educational deprivation rarely exists by itself: in general, those without education are also far poorer than those who have completed high school or college. The median income for a family whose head did not get past grade school is about $6,500. For those who have finished high school, the median income is close to $9,000, and for those who finished college, it is almost $13,000. But in the *Newsweek* poll, education level was more influential in middle America's thinking than any other single factor.

The effect of education on thinking showed up on almost every fundamental issue:

§ Confidence in the country: Half the college group and only 25 per cent of the grade school group were more confident about the country's ability to solve its problems than they had been five years ago; 52 per cent of the grade school group were less confident. Forty-two per cent of the college group and 24 per cent of the grade school group thought the country had changed for the better.

Q. COMPARED WITH FIVE YEARS AGO, DO YOU FEEL MORE
CONFIDENT OR LESS CONFIDENT ABOUT THE ABILITY OF
THIS COUNTRY TO SOLVE ITS PROBLEMS?

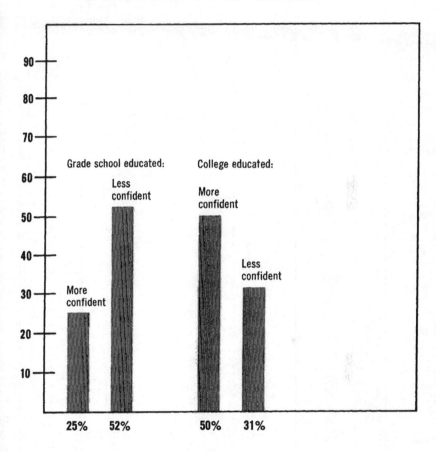

Q.   COMPARING THIS COUNTRY WITH WHAT IT WAS LIKE
      TEN YEARS AGO, DO YOU THINK THIS COUNTRY HAS
      CHANGED FOR THE BETTER OR FOR THE WORSE?

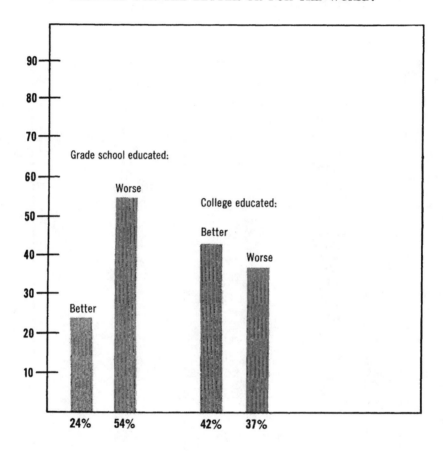

§ Personal prosperity: 43 per cent of the college group and 24 per cent of the grade school group said they were better off than they were five years ago. Twice as many of the college group expected to be better off five years from now.

§ Civil rights: 44 per cent of the college group and 24 per cent of the grade school group listed civil rights as one of the country's three major problems.

§ The Negro's chances: The college group divided evenly over whether the Negro had a better chance (37 per cent) or a worse chance (36 per cent) of getting a good job than they did, but 58 per cent of the grade school group thought the Negro's chances were better, and only 10 per cent thought they were worse. On the question of getting a good education, 37 per cent of the college group thought they were better and 26 per cent thought they were worse, while 54 per cent of the grade school group thought they were better and only 4 per cent thought they were worse.

§ The Negro's ability to help himself: 58 per cent of the college group thought the Negro could have done something about his slums and 22 per cent thought he couldn't have; 80 per cent of the grade school group felt he could have helped himself and 7 per cent felt he couldn't.

§ Negro demands: 85 per cent of the college group and 56 per cent of the grade school group saw at least some justification in them.

§ George Wallace: 79 per cent of the college group and 53 per cent of the grade school group thought the country would be worse off with Wallace as President.

§ Vietnam: surprisingly, 33 per cent of the grade school group and only 16 per cent of the college group said that American troops should never have gone into Vietnam.

§ Young people: two-thirds of the college group looked favorably on the young people of today and only 15 per cent felt unfavorable; the grade school group was evenly split, 34 per cent favorable and 33 per cent unfavorable.

Q.   IN YOUR OPINION, DO NEGROES TODAY HAVE A BETTER
     CHANCE OR A WORSE CHANCE THAN PEOPLE LIKE YOUR-
     SELF TO GET A WELL-PAYING JOB?

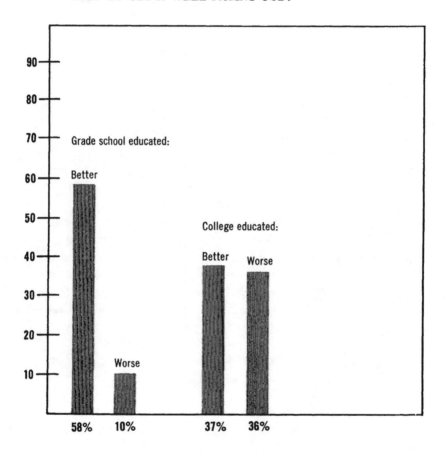

Q. IN YOUR OPINION, DO NEGROES TODAY HAVE A BETTER
    CHANCE OR A WORSE CHANCE THAN PEOPLE LIKE YOUR-
    SELF TO GET A GOOD EDUCATION FOR THEIR CHILDREN?

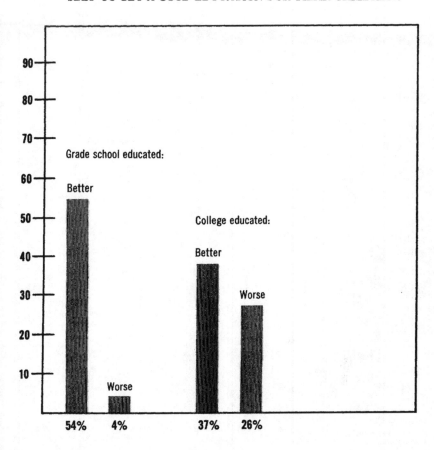

Q. IN YOUR OPINION, DO NEGROES TODAY HAVE A BETTER CHANCE OR A WORSE CHANCE THAN PEOPLE LIKE YOUR-SELF TO GET GOOD HOUSING AT A REASONABLE COST?

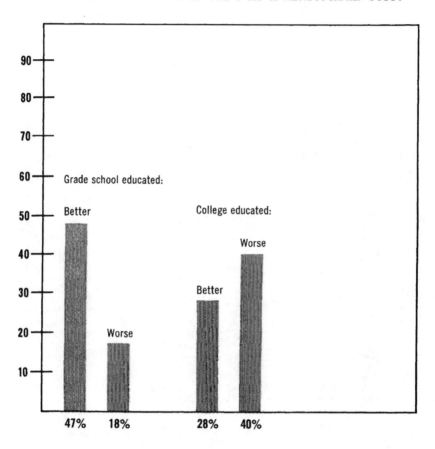

Q. IN YOUR OPINION, DO NEGROES TODAY HAVE A BETTER CHANCE OR A WORSE CHANCE THAN PEOPLE LIKE YOURSELF TO GET FINANCIAL HELP FROM THE GOVERNMENT WHEN THEY'RE OUT OF WORK?

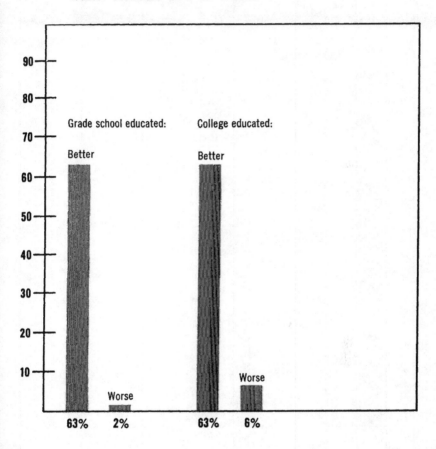

Q. DO YOU THINK THAT CONDITIONS THAT NEGROES HAVE
HAD TO LIVE WITH IN THE SLUMS ARE SOMETHING THEY
HAVE HAD TO PUT UP WITH, OR COULD THEY HAVE
DONE SOMETHING ABOUT THESE CONDITIONS THEM-
SELVES?

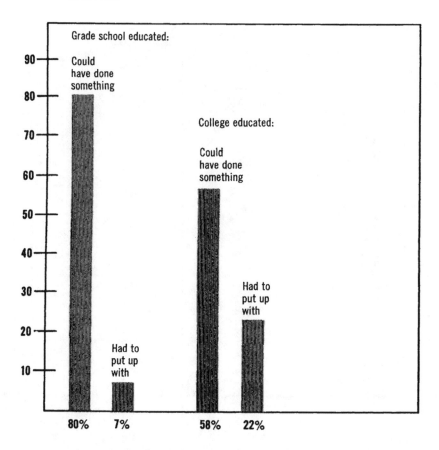

Q. WHICH ONE STATEMENT ON THIS CARD BEST DESCRIBES
   YOUR FEELINGS ABOUT THE DEMANDS BEING MADE BY
   NEGRO LEADERS THESE DAYS?

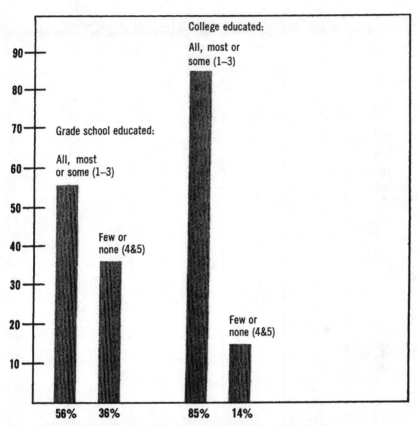

1. These demands are completely justified and should be met right away.
2. Most of these demands are justified, but it will take some time to meet them.
3. Some of these demands are justified, but it will take some time to meet them.
4. Very few of these demands are justified, and they have pretty much been taken care of.
5. These demands are completely unjustified and they should not be granted.

Q. WOULD YOU PLEASE READ CAREFULLY ALL THE STATE-
MENTS ON THIS CARD. WHICH ONE OF THE STATEMENTS
COMES CLOSEST TO YOUR FEELINGS ABOUT THE WAR IN
VIETNAM?

We had no right or reason to send our troops to fight in Vietnam in the first place:

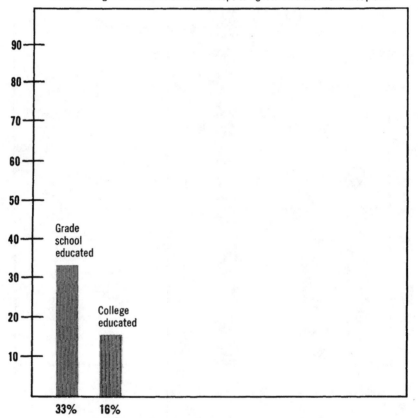

Q. IS YOUR OPINION OF MOST YOUNG PEOPLE TODAY FAVORABLE OR UNFAVORABLE?

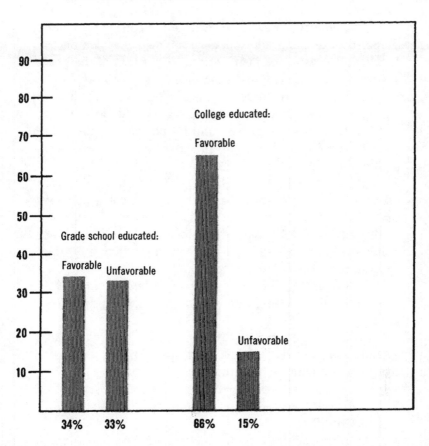

§ Criticism by the young: 62 per cent of the college group and 44 per cent of the grade school group said criticism was needed.

§ Demonstrators: 53 per cent of the college group and 22 per cent of the grade school group said that demonstrators have at least some justification; 71 per cent of the grade school group said they had little or no justification.

§ The goals for today's youth: 62 per cent of the college group said that a young person should do what he wanted, regardless of money, and 64 per cent of the grade school group said he should get an education for a well-paying job.

§ Taxes: both groups thought federal taxes were too high, but criticism of local taxes increased as education level decreased: 45 per cent of the college group and 70 per cent of the grade school group found local taxes too high. The grade school group was also more inclined than any other to use a surplus to reduce taxes.

§ Space: 74 per cent of the grade school group and 39 per cent of the college group would spend less on space programs.

§ Trust in the media: 58 per cent of the grade school group and 73 per cent of the college group put at least some trust in the media's truthfulness.

§ Materialism: 54 per cent of the college group and 36 per cent of the grade school group said that the U. S. is too materialistic.

§ The need for experimentation: 53 per cent of the college group and 30 per cent of the grade school group endorsed experimentation in dealing with the nation's problems.

§ Nudity and sex: 49 per cent of the college group and 71 per cent of the grade school group thought they were undermining America's morals a great deal.

The extent of these differences is sobering in itself, but the two educational groups differed more often and by wider margins that any other groups in the *Newsweek* sample.

Q. SOME PEOPLE SAY YOUNG PEOPLE ARE TOO CRITICAL TODAY ABOUT THIS COUNTRY. OTHERS SAY THIS CRITICISM IS NEEDED AND SHOULD BE KEPT UP. WHICH SIDE DO YOU AGREE WITH MORE?

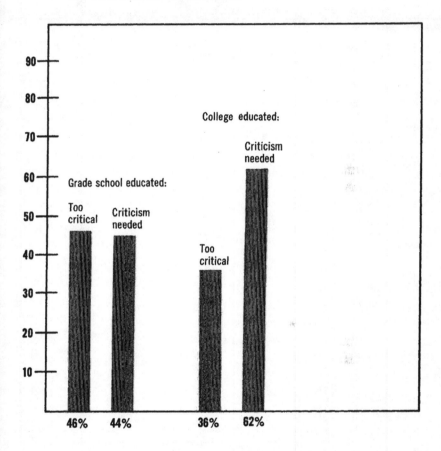

Q.   TO WHAT EXTENT DO YOU THINK THE MORALS OF THIS
     COUNTRY ARE BEING UNDERMINED BY THE CURRENT
     EMPHASIS ON SEX AND NUDITY IN THE MOVIES, THEA-
     TERS, BOOKS, AND MAGAZINES—A GREAT DEAL, SOME,
     A LITTLE, OR NOT AT ALL?

A great deal:

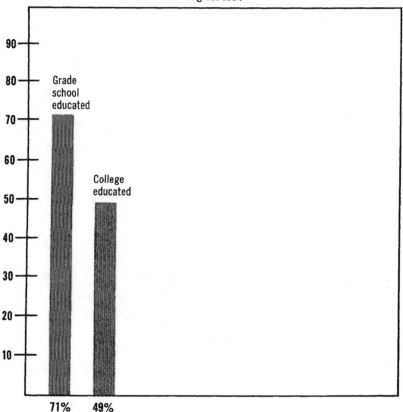

71%   49%

On 20 questions where substantial differences between groups occurred, the college–grade school split was compared with the splits between white collar and blue collar workers, the old and the young, and, at the economic extremes *outside* middle America, the rich and the poor. In 58 of these 60 comparisons, the educational split was larger than any other. On all 20 questions, the difference based on educational level was greater than the difference based on age and occupation, and on 19 of the 20 the difference was greater than that based on income. There was a greater split between the rich and the poor on trust in the media, and the difference between rich and poor on George Wallace was the same as that between the education groups.

On many of these questions, moreover, the education split was *substantially* greater than the split between any other groups. On the question of materialism, for example, the college educated and the grade school educated were separated by 18 per cent; the old and the young were separated by only 6 per cent, the white collar-blue collar groups by 4 per cent, and the rich and the poor by 1 per cent. On the question of confidence in the country, the college–grade school difference was 26 per cent; the young and the old differed by 15 per cent, the rich and the poor by 10 per cent, and the blue collar and white collar by 10 per cent. On the question of whether Negro demands are justified, the college–grade school difference was 29 per cent; the rich and poor differed by 23 per cent, the white collar and blue collar by 12 per cent, and the young and old by 6 per cent. The same pattern held true on questions about the Negro's chances, whether the Negro could have helped himself, the young, college demonstrators, the need for criticism, the need for experimentation, the effects of sex and nudity, the goals of the young, whether the country was better or worse, and whether or not people care about strangers.

Great as these differences are, the differences between the extreme ends of the two educational groups is greater still. At one end, America's colleges and universities are spawning a new breed of activist intellectuals who see little merit in "the system" and want to scrap it. At the other end, those with only grade school educations are the staunchest and angriest defenders of the system. These extremists set the tone of encounters, and they represent the cutting edge of discontent.

Within the middle American sample, The Gallup Organization compared the 54 per cent of the grade school educated who said that the country was changing for the worse with the blue collar workers, white collar workers, old, and poor who also believed the country was getting worse. The grade school group emerged as the most pessimistic of all the pessimists. They felt less confident than any other group about the country's ability to handle its problems. They felt the least prosperous; 45 per cent of the grade school pessimists and 35 per cent of the blue collar pessimists said things were worse for people like themselves than they had been five years ago. They were the most resentful of the black man. Fifty-four per cent of the blue collar group said that Negroes had a better chance for a good job than they did, but 65 per cent of the grade school group thought his chances were better. They were the most tolerant of George Wallace. Of all the middle Americans who felt the country had changed for the worse, 63 per cent said it would be worse still under Wallace; 66 per cent of the old group and 60 per cent of the blue collar group said it would be worse; but among the grade school group, only 47 per cent said the country would be worse off under Wallace. They had the least sympathy with the war in Vietnam; 33 per cent said America should never have gone there, almost twice the percentage of any other group.

They were the most down on today's young people. Among the middle Americans who felt the country had changed for the worse, 51 per cent had a favorable opinion of the young; in the blue collar group, 46 per cent were favorable. In the grade school group, only 28 per cent were favorable while 36 per cent were unfavorable, and they were the only group in which those who were unfavorable were in the majority. They had the least use for college demonstrators: *none* of them felt the demonstrators were justified completely or in large part. They were more inclined than any other group to want more money spent on social security and old age benefits. And they felt more strongly than any other group that sex and nudity were seriously undermining the nation's morals.

In trying to predict the future mood of the nation, many observers have stressed that the population is growing younger and better educated. The implications of increasing youthfulness are complex and difficult to define: many young people in the working class are no more liberal than their parents. But the implications of improving education seem clear. Three-quarters of those 75 years old and older have had less than four years of high school. Only 14 per cent of them completed high school, and only 11 per cent had any college. Among 20- and 21-year-olds, only 18 per cent have had *less* than four years of high school, while 42 per cent finished high school and 40 per cent have been to college. The education level of Americans increases in inverse proportion to age for all age groups: Among those 35 to 44 years old, 34 per cent had less than four years of high school, while 41 per cent completed it and 25 per cent went on to college. Today, 78 per cent of all white males have at least finished high school, compared to 65 per cent just ten years ago, and 60 per cent of all Negro males have at least finished high school, compared to only 36 per cent ten years ago.

Similarly, the white collar group in America is growing much more rapidly than the blue collar group. Since 1950, the number of male white collar workers has jumped from 13.5 million to more than 19 million, while the number of blue collar workers has increased from 19.7 million to 22.8 million.

These figures spell out some important facts about middle America's future. Those who are most angry, most alienated, and most traditional are dwindling in numbers, while the least angry, alienated and traditional are growing steadily. But there is small comfort in that when most of the middle Americans are angry to one degree or another, and even the improving educational picture presents America with a problem: it will have to decide what to do with those who are left behind.

10

PEOPLE
LIKE US

George Layos was frying eggs behind the counter of the Nuttie Foodie Tea Room on Main Street in Springfield, Massachusetts.

"I've never collected a day of welfare in my life," he said. "In my family, if you stay home and don't work, you're a bum and a criminal. These black guys think they've got it tough. When my father came to this country from Greece in 1910, he could speak five languages. People laughed at him and called him stupid. There's plenty of work around, these people just don't have backbone. They give them welfare just to keep them quiet. The police aren't tough enough. They're scared. I get nervous, too. Ten years ago, if somebody came in here and gave me some baloney, I'd throw his ass out. Today, you never know if they're hopped up on dope or something. I see them take candy out of the counter and I just let them go. You never know what they're going to do. If you and I stole a doughnut, we'd be put in jail. But they walk out with TV sets and the police are afraid to do anything about it." Down the street, on the box office of the rundown Paramount Theater, a sign reads, "No one will be allowed in the theater without shoes on their feet."

Ernest (Pee Wee) Hayes is 58, and for 37 years he has worked at the Armco steel plant in Middletown, Ohio. His father migrated north from Kentucky during the Depression, and when Hayes started work, he earned $3.85 for an eight-hour day. Now he gets $3.69 an hour and more than $10,000 a year. He has money in the company credit union and gets four weeks of vacation a year, and 13 weeks every fifth year. He owns a freezer, a fairly new Buick, and most of the $15,000 house which he bought for $5,300 twenty years ago. The company pays all his expenses in a gun club and there is a generous retirement plan. But for most of his working life, he has stood in the same 12-foot-square area, operating a machine that shears rough edges off long lengths of steel.

"The older you get the worse it gets," Hayes said dolefully. "The pressure and tension keep building up. More tonnage. You get behind the 8-ball. I've worked hard. I've wore out three machines. We do all the work and the niggers have got it made. They keep closing in and closing in, working their way into everything. Last three or four months you can't even turn on that damn TV without seeing a nigger. They're even playing cowboys. Us Briarhoppers ain't gonna stand for it. And ninety per cent of Middletown is Briarhoppers. And those sons-of-bitches will kill you, know what I mean? If a bunch of good ole Briarhopper Ku Kluxers had got ahold of Martin Luther King, he wouldn't have lived as long as he did. I have a half dozen guns and they ain't gonna be registered. Those sons-of-bitches wanting something for nothing would knock your head off for a nickel. The law told me that if you shoot one of them, drag him in the house, don't leave him out in the yard.

"My man got beat, Wallace. We need someone to wake

'em up. Shake 'em up. Kill 'em. Sons-of-bitches try to run everything, and they can't run nothin'."

"Come on, Pee Wee," one of his colleagues objected. "There are some good colored people, probably better than I am."

"You say there are niggers better than you?" Hayes asked in surprise.

"You're damned right."

"Well, I'm a son-of-a-bitch," Hayes said, incredulously. "I'd never say that if I lived to be a hundred and fifty years old."

In a carpeted, brightly lit clothing store in Portland, Oregon, 54-year-old Jerry Semler, who wears sideburns and a mustache, was bantering with a customer. "I'm just a shoe dog," he said. "I've been peddling shoes all my life. And in this business, if you're not happy, you're dead. I'd possibly like to do something else, but I don't know what it would be. I love my wife. I've got three fine children. I've got a nice house in a middle class neighborhood. Friends come over and we turn off the boob tube and talk. I get two weeks' vacation a year—I go up to Lake Tahoe and booze it up a little. I'm my own man. I had a heart attack in 1956, at 12:10, September 30, sitting in a green chair. But whoever pulls the cards out of the rack upstairs wasn't ready to pull mine. I'm active as I ever was. The one big thing that bothers me is the war. It just galls me every time some one is killed. Billions and billions of dollars, and I don't know how many have been killed, but you can't kill an idea. To pull their chestnuts out of the fire with the lives of our boys—unh-uh."

At the huge, austere New England insurance company compound, television cameras inspect the cars and people arriving at the security gate. Inside, there are 2,100 employees (of whom 1,400 are women), a company store, a bank, a credit union, an inexpensive lunch room, and many recreational facilities.

"It's a womb to tomb life," said one supervisor. "They lead you in the bathroom. You piddle. And then you go back and do your job. It becomes frustrating. You go home wondering, 'What the hell did I do today?' Sometimes I'd like to see some good come of what I did in a day. But you're such a small cog in such a big wheel that it all gets lost in the whole mishmash. There's you and your family, and that's your world. If your neighbor dies tomorrow, just throw a little sand on him and that's about it. People don't want to get involved. Everybody's concern is not to be concerned."

Senior mechanic Bill Scudder finished repairing a leak in the aileron-boost system of a Piedmont Airlines jet at the Atlanta airport and wiped his hands. Scudder is 33, feeds four children on an $820 a month salary, and manages to put away $80 a month in the company credit union. He lives in the country, fifteen miles from his job, and his wife bakes bread and cakes and cans beans, tomatoes, and okra from a summer garden on their small lot. They chip in with neighbors to buy potatoes and meat in bulk at wholesale prices. One neighbor helped Scudder get some used plumbing and he added a bathroom in the basement of his house for $40. For recreation, the family camps, and they are deeply involved in the church and the Scouts.

"I guess I've been too busy to sit down and figure out what my problems are," Scudder said. "I'm happy. Cities make me nervous. Country people are outgoing and friendly, but city life keeps people so tense they don't want to talk to anybody. All I want out of life is for my kids to grow up to be decent citizens. I'm happy with my family, so I'm happy with the world. All I need to do is wake up in the morning and hear the birds sing. That gives me joy."

At a weekend carnival on the grounds of a dingy, old high school in Hammond, Indiana, steelworker Jimmy Slavo, 57, was strolling about, holding hands with his wife Lula Belle, drinking a Budweiser, and dipping Copenhagen snuff.

Slavo has been working in the steel mills in Hammond since 1928, and he earns $3.67 an hour as a steel pourer. His wife has been sick, and he owes $7,000 in medical bills, so he tries to work a lot of overtime, but the temperature where he works averages 115 degrees and he can't put in the hours he'd like. "I sweat so much salt that when I undress, my pants stand up by themselves," he says. "The heat knocks you on your hind end." "The heat seems to give him power," his wife says proudly. To help feed and clothe their three children, Lula Belle Slavo bakes and sews, and they keep a tiny garden in the summer. They got a freezer four years ago, hoping to buy bulk foodstuffs and save money, but for lack of cash they have only been able to fill it twice. Slavo has never been on an airplane or in a nightclub, and for vacation, the Slavos visit relatives in Minnesota. They haven't been to a movie in ten years. Lula Belle Slavo said the last time she went out to dinner was on her birthday three years ago. She had fried chicken.

"Guys on relief are a lot happier," Jimmy Slavo said. "They got cars. They got food. I work, and what the hell have I got? A bunch of bills and a wife and kids to take care of. There are too many goddam people doing nothing and getting paid for it. I can't ask for charity. But why the hell should they soak the little man? I never did get any help from anybody. I'd be ashamed to ask. I'm too damn proud. I'll pay my bills. Anyway, to hell with the money. I've still got my wife. If sickness would stay away, we'd be happy. All I care about is my family," he concluded, and squeezed his wife's hand affectionately.

Mrs. Emma Riel lives in one of the valleys outside Los Angeles, and sews and makes plastic flowers to supplement her husband's $10,000 a year income as a sewer equipment salesman. In her front yard, an American flag is mounted on a white picket fence, and a wire fence separates her from her neighbor.

"Everybody wants the same thing—decency—but people like us don't count for anything any more," Emma Riel said angrily. "One woman can stop prayer in the schools. And a man with a prison record is patted on the head and told to do it again. Mr. [Earl] Warren handcuffed our police, and our laws are not protecting anyone. I'm not scared to walk the street, but nine-tenths of the women around here are. People are more afraid than you'll ever know, and they're unhappy. We're losing what we had to preserve. We can no longer go before other nations and stand proud. We're ashamed. Our politicians aren't truthful. And the kids— they want it all right now, the things it took us a lifetime to get. A bath, a haircut, and a good, old-fashioned strap would get most of them back in line. But their mothers are too busy at cocktail parties and bridge clubs to be mothers."

"People like us need a lobby in Washington," said Mrs. Lorraine Lindahl, a graying mother of six in Minneapolis. "All the government wants from us is our money and our boys to send to Vietnam. They don't give a cotton-picking goldarn about anything else."

Middle America is not one place, one set of people, or one frame of mind. It is scattered all across America, and its inhabitants are sometimes cheerful, sometimes bitter, sometimes angry, sometimes apathetic, and sometimes just satisfied. But the dominant strain in middle America now is one of resentment at both real and fancied neglect, and it has eaten dangerously far into the traditional spirit of America's common people. Often this resentment bursts out as mean-spirited and self-pitying. "When 'Middle American' stops feeling sorry for himself, and stops using others as his excuse for failure, we may again get on with progress 'toward a more perfect Union!' " one man who called himself a middle American wrote *Newsweek*. At other times the resentment comes out in the form of hatred, bigotry, fear, worry, anger, or resignation. Whatever form it takes, it is an emotion no country can afford in quantity for very long, but getting rid of it will require open-mindedness and determination in middle America and outside it.

"We must rethink all our old ideas and beliefs before they capture and destroy us," Robert F. Kennedy said, and that is true both of middle America and of those who judge middle America. When all complaints and accusations have been considered, Americans are left with the basic fact that theirs is the richest and freest country in the world, and they have little reason or excuse for not making it the happiest. They can't abolish factionalism or hatred or injustice, but they can resist these inevitable flaws and they can regain the boldness, perhaps only temporarily misplaced, which they once thought the country was all about. That spirit set strange forces in motion, and America must reckon with them now, but it is too late to call off the experiment. The hope for America is that few people really want to call it off, and that, buffeted by change as they are, they can regain their celebrated confidence in the future and the itch to get on with it.

It seems astonishing that many Americans don't love the future any more. For many years, it was their special time. Europe had the past, but the future belonged to Americans, and they were full of plans about what they would do with it: open up the West, harness huge rivers, send up gleaming new buildings, and show the world what a country could do when it started from scratch. But at least for now, America has broken off its love affair with the future. The people no longer feel confident about what it holds in store, and they are sick of its fickleness and fancy ways. They want a little peace and permanence.

That may well change: in the long run, Americans will clearly have to change either their minds or their character, or both. Even in their present disgruntlement, they have their tranquil and confident voices. "We just won't sit around and let the country go down the drain," says a young aircraft inspector in California; and a young machinist in New Jersey says assuringly, "We'll find a way." Such voices may become a majority again.

But it seems likely that America will have to look for a way that is in many respects different from the old one, because that way no longer makes people happy. It doesn't satisfy many of the young, who find it too narrow, and it doesn't satisfy the old-fashioned, who find that it is producing a noisier, uglier, more jarring world than it was supposed to. Yet the new way will have to grow out of the old one if the country does not want to alienate a great number of its people. Almost nobody so far has any specific remedies for dealing with America's new discontent, but if a way is found, it probably will be by applying the old spirit which most Americans cherish to the new problems which they have come to fear. It will come, that is, when the people get back their old love of the future, their old, brazen confidence which Carl Sandburg, the people's poet, so admired:

> I speak of new cities and new people.
> I tell you the past is a bucket of ashes.
> I tell you yesterday is a world gone down,
>   a sun dropped into the West.
> I tell you there is nothing in the world
>   only an ocean of tomorrow, a sky of
>   tomorrows.

When those words were written, there was nothing nostalgic about the American dream. It was a dream of the future, based on the conviction that tomorrow would be better. Today, many Americans expect the future to be a bucket of ashes, and the world they yearn for is a world gone down. They have lost the old spirit by yearning for the old ways. But the American dream was always predicated on the conviction that the future was controlled by the people, and many middle Americans have come to dislike change because they no longer feel they have any say in the way it affects them. Their challenge to the system and themselves, therefore, is simply to regain the time-honored role of the American people: not to resist change but to insist upon it, which means insisting on taking part in the process by which changes are made. The silent majority was supposed to be satisfied and proud; the one clear lesson of its discontent is that a silent majority and government by the people are incompatible.

APPENDIX A:

THE
QUESTIONNAIRE

NATIONAL OPINION SURVEY
THE GALLUP ORGANIZATION, INC.
PRINCETON, NEW JERSEY

INTRODUCTION:
I'm taking a Gallup Survey and I'd like your opinion on some leading topics of the day. Here's the first question I'd like to ask you . . .

1. What do you think are the two or three most important problems facing the nation today?

	per cent
Vietnam	63.6
Taxes	18.0
Poverty	17.4
Youth protests	13.8
International problems	3.0
Communism	1.2
Morality and religion	5.4
Civil rights (including related items)	41.3
High cost of living	26.0
Crime and delinquency	9.9
Peace, bomb	2.2
Russia-China	0.4
National defense	0.8

2. What do you think are the two or three most important problems facing the people of this particular community today?

	per cent
High taxes	18.1
Civil rights, race problems	13.9
Transportation	9.0
Crime	6.5
Youth problems, delinquency	7.6
Morality and religion	1.6
Inflation	15.1
Education	12.0
Housing	8.9
Welfare	3.2
No problems	8.5

3. Compared with five years ago, do you feel more confident or less confident about the ability of this country to solve its problems?

	per cent
More confident	40.1
Less confident	40.2
No difference	15.8
Don't know	3.9

4. Compared with five years ago, would you say things for people like yourself and your family are better, worse, or about the same?

	per cent
Better	36.3
Worse	24.9
Same	37.0
Don't know	1.7

5. Thinking ahead to five years from now, would you say things for people like yourself and your family will be better, worse or about the same as they are now?

	per cent
Better	34.1
Worse	28.0
Same	30.0
Don't know	8.0

6. (HAND RESPONDENT CARD A) On which of the items on this card would you say the U. S. has changed for the better, and on which would you say it has changed for the worse?

	per cent	
	BETTER	WORSE
Standards of morality	10.3	77.0
Opportunities for people like yourself to get ahead	60.1	15.8
Providing good medical care for people like yourself and your family	59.4	20.5
Providing good housing at reasonable costs for people like yourself and your family	21.2	53.9
Providing financial security in your old age for people like yourself and your family	59.8	21.5
None of them	5.2	4.5
Don't know	4.0	3.2

7. In your opinion, do Negroes today have a better chance or a worse chance than people like yourself:

	per cent			
	BETTER	WORSE	SAME	DON'T KNOW
To get well-paying jobs?	43.6	21.2	31.1	4.1
To get a good education for their children?	41.3	15.5	40.5	2.7
To get good housing at a reasonable cost?	34.6	30.4	27.4	7.6
To get financial help from the government when they're out of work?	64.8	4.1	21.5	9.6

8. Do you think most people today are more religious or less religious than they were five years ago?

	per cent
More religious	10.5
Less religious	69.8
No difference	16.5
Don't know	3.3

9. How many people today do you think really care about what happens to people they don't know personally—Do most people care, about half, some, or hardly anybody?

	per cent
Most	16.3
About half	22.6
Some	26.3
Hardly anybody	32.8
Don't know	1.9

10a. (HAND RESPONDENT SCALE) You notice the rungs on this ladder go all the way from 10, for something you rate very *favorably,* all the way down to 0, for something you rate very unfavorably. How far up, or how far down, this ladder would you rate the way Nixon is handling his job as President?

	per cent
7 - 10	49.0
5 - 8	61.3
5 - 6	31.1
0 - 4	15.4

10b. Why do you give him that rating?

	per cent
FAVORABLE	
Working for peace	11.3
Done well so far	5.0
Trying to solve problems	9.2
Just generally OK	11.1
UNFAVORABLE	
Has not kept promises	4.7
Disapprove of Vietnam	2.4
Generally unfavorable	4.7

11. Suppose Hubert Humphrey had been elected President last year. Do you think this country would be better off or worse off than it is now?

	per cent
Better	10.2
Worse	39.5
No difference	39.7
Don't know	10.5

12. And suppose George Wallace had been elected President last year. Do you think this country would be better off or worse off than it is now?

	per cent
Better	11.8
Worse	67.9
No difference	9.3
Don't know	11.1

13. What is your opinion about the way we have fought the war in Vietnam?

	per cent
Should never have gone	16.8
Get out or go all out	6.8
Too many killed	10.3
Pull out	6.2
Needed more aggressiveness	11.3
Badly managed	16.3
Should be over	12.6
General knocks	14.3

14. Would you please read carefully all the statements on this card. (HAND RESPONDENT CARD B) Which *one* of the statements comes closest to your feelings about the war in Vietnam?

	per cent
It was our right and duty to send our troops to Vietnam to fight the communists.	25.7
While we were justified in sending our troops to Vietnam, it would have been better if we had only sent military aid and supplies.	32.3
Even though we had some reasons for sending our troops to Vietnam, everything considered we should have stayed out.	18.7
We had no right or reason to send our troops to fight in Vietnam in the first place.	19.0
No opinion	4.3

15. As you know, U.S. troops have been fighting in Vietnam since 1963. All things considered since then, would you say we are winning the war in Vietnam, losing it, or holding our own?

	per cent
Winning	8.3
Losing	19.6
Holding own	66.3
No opinion	5.8

16. Do you know personally anyone who has been wounded or killed in Vietnam?

	per cent
Yes	55.1
No	44.7

On the next topic . . .

17. Is your opinion of most young people today favorable or unfavorable?

	per cent
Favorable	58.5
Unfavorable	19.0
Mixed	20.2
Don't know	2.3

18. Why do you say that?

	per cent
FAVORABLE:	
Majority are good	20.3
Only bad are publicized	8.8
Had favorable experience	10.5
More educated, intelligent	9.1
Involved, concerned	7.9
UNFAVORABLE:	
Don't take responsibility	2.4
Drugs	1.9
Hippies	1.9
Dress	1.9
Morality and religion	1.9
No respect for authority	1.8
No respect for elders	1.4
Riots, etc.	1.7
Wild, undisciplined	1.9
Parents' fault	1.6

19. (HAND RESPONDENT CARD C) Which *one* statement on this card comes closest to your opinion about how to deal with the demands of Negroes for better education?

	per cent
Ignore them because they are not justified	3.2
Improve schools where Negro children go	39.8
Move in the direction of integrating white and black schools	24.7
Integrate schools by busing school children	1.6
Allow Negroes to run and control their own schools	24.0
Don't know	6.8

20. What is your impression—is the danger of racial violence in U.S. cities increasing or decreasing?

	per cent
Increasing	58.5
Decreasing	26.0
Remaining same	11.5
No opinion	4.0

21. Why do you think that is the case?

	per cent
INCREASING:	
Negroes want too much	9.5
More militant	6.5
Negro leaders	3.7
Too much power	1.2
Communists	1.5
Violence worked in past	2.8
Want more than whites	2.3
Too much violence	3.8
News shows violence	6.3
Demands not met yet	5.3
Not getting fair deal	2.1
Conditions not improved	2.9
Bigotry	1.9
Laws not tough enough	4.4
DECREASING:	
Less violent now	9.5
Demands being met	3.7
Better relations	3.4

On another topic . . .

22. (HAND RESPONDENT CARD D) Which two or three of the problems on this card do you think are the most serious ones facing people who live in cities?

	per cent
The number of people on welfare	42.0
Air pollution	31.9
Water pollution	13.0
Lack of decent housing at a reasonable cost	34.3
The quality of transportation to and from work	6.1
Use of drugs	43.3
Strikes by city employees	8.4
Crimes of violence	63.6
Racial problems	43.7
Don't know	.4

23. How many people on welfare today do you think could earn their own way if they really wanted to—most of them, about half, some, or hardly anybody?

	per cent
Most of them	38.1
About half	41.1
Some	17.6
Hardly anybody	2.1
Don't know	1.0

24. Are the schools in this community doing a good job, a fair job, or a poor job when it comes to:

	per cent			
	GOOD	FAIR	POOR	DON'T KNOW
Giving children a good quality education?	64.2	22.9	5.6	7.2
Helping children to become mature responsible citizens?	54.2	28.3	9.2	8.3
Preparing young people for good jobs?	56.7	27.3	7.3	8.7

25. What do you think of young people and college students who are involved in demonstrations and sit-ins? Are they completely justified in their actions, in large part justified, to some degree, very little, or not at all?

	per cent
Completely	1.0
In large part	4.9
To some degree	34.4
Very little	26.2
Not at all	31.1
Don't know	2.4

On the next topic . . .

26. The phrase "law and order" means different things to different people. When you hear the phrase "law and order" what comes to mind? Anything else?

	per cent
Respect for law and order	56.7
More law enforcement	20.2
Police (positive)	11.3
Riots and demonstrations	4.1
Protection, safety, peace	16.3

27. Do you think the police in this area do a good job or not so good job of preventing crime in this neighborhood?

	per cent
Good job	78.1
Not so good	15.8
Don't know	6.1

28. How serious a problem in this community do you think the use of drugs by young people is today—very serious, fairly serious, not too serious, or not at all serious?

	per cent
Very serious	24.9
Fairly serious	22.2
Not too serious	26.3
Not at all serious	17.6
Don't know	9.1

29. How serious a problem in this community do you think violent crimes like mugging and burglary is today—very serious, fairly serious, not too serious, or not at all serious?

	per cent
Very serious	18.7
Fairly serious	23.2
Not too serious	37.3
Not at all serious	19.0
Don't know	1.7

30. In your opinion, do the police today have too little power, too much power, or about the right amount in dealing with persons suspected of having committed a crime?

	per cent
Too little power	62.6
Too much power	3.1
About the right amount	32.0
Don't know	2.4

31. Suppose you were being robbed while walking at night in this neighborhood. How likely do you think it is that people would come to your help—very likely, fairly likely, not too likely, or not at all likely?

	per cent
Very likely	29.8
Fairly likely	29.8
Not too likely	20.4
Not at all likely	17.2
Don't know	2.7

32a. Have you or any member of your family living here changed your habits in any way because of a possible danger from criminals?

	per cent
Yes	28.9
No	71.1

(If *Yes*, ask b)

32b. Would you please tell me in what way:

	per cent
Lock doors, windows	17.7
Worry when out at night	9.3
Have gun	3.6
Have dog	1.6
Burglar alarm	0.3

Turning to another subject . . .

33. Compared with five years ago, are you and your family able to buy more and better things than you did then, are you having to cut back on what you buy, or are you living just about the same as you did then?

	per cent
Buying more	29.0
Cutting back	25.3
About same	44.4
Don't know	1.2

34. Comparing this country with what it was like ten years ago, do you think this country has changed for the better or for the worse?

	per cent
Better	36.0
Worse	46.0
No difference	12.0
Don't know	4.8

35. How much danger do you think there is that in the years ahead this country might be changed for the worse—considerable danger, a fair amount, little, or hardly any at all?

	per cent
Considerable	26.5
Fair amount	31.7
Little	18.5
Hardly at all	14.2
Don't know	9.1

36. Would you say the taxes you pay to the federal government in Washington are too high, too low, or about right?

per cent			
TOO HIGH	ABOUT RIGHT	TOO LOW	DON'T KNOW
77.8	21.1	0.1	1.0

37. Would you say the taxes you pay to the local county or city government are too high, too low, or about right?

per cent			
TOO HIGH	ABOUT RIGHT	TOO LOW	DON'T KNOW
59.3	36.2	1.0	3.4

38. Suppose the federal government in Washington found it had collected more money in taxes than it had expected. It could use this money to reduce the national debt, it could reduce taxes, or it could use this money to improve conditions in this country. Which *one* of these would you favor most?

	per cent
Reduce debt	15.8
Reduce taxes	33.8
Improve conditions	48.1
Don't know	2.3

39. (HAND RESPONDENT CARD E) On which, if any, of the items on this list do you think the government should be spending *more* money than it is now? Any others? (RECORD BELOW.)

40. (HAND RESPONDENT CARD E) On which, if any, do you think the government should be spending *less* money than it is now? Any others? (RECORD BELOW.)

	per cent	
	Q. 39 MORE	Q. 40 LESS
Space exploration to the moon, Mars, etc.	9.7	55.7
Air and water pollution	55.8	3.3
Social security benefits	46.1	5.6
Medicare for the old and needy	47.0	4.6
Provide better housing for the poor, particularly in the black ghettoes	39.4	12.6
Improve schools	43.6	6.9
Military aid to foreign countries	1.2	65.7
Economic aid to foreign countries	5.6	56.7
Military expenditures for defense	15.6	26.2
Job training for the unemployed	56.3	7.1
Building highways	23.0	14.3
Providing public transportation (buses and trains)	20.2	16.0
Do something about organized crime such as that committed by gangsters and racketeers	54.8	3.3
Do something about crimes such as muggings, burglaries	44.3	3.7
None of them	1.4	2.7
Don't know	0.7	2.8

41. Do you think that conditions that Negroes have had to live with in the slums are something they have had to put up with, or

could they have done something about these conditions themselves?

	per cent
Put up with	12.5
Could have done something	72.7
Both	13.0
Don't know	1.8

42. Do you think the high unemployment rate among Negroes is something they could have done something about themselves, or is it the result of discrimination in education and hiring?

	per cent
Could have done something	54.8
Discrimination	21.2
Both	21.2
Don't know	2.8

On the next topic . . .

43. When a person is arrested on suspicion of having committed a crime, if he can get money to put up bail, he is allowed to go free until his trial. Some people say judges should have the right to deny bail when they feel a person might commit a crime before he came to trial. Other people oppose this because they feel this is like convicting a man before he comes to trial. Which side do you agree with more?

	per cent
Judge should be able to deny bail	67.7
Oppose this	23.4
Don't know	8.9

44. How much do you think the federal government in Washington can be trusted to tell the truth about what is going on in the world today—can it be trusted a great deal, some, little, or not at all?

	per cent
A great deal	13.2
Some	51.3
Little	24.0
Not at all	8.4
Don't know	3.0

45. And how much do you think that newspapers, magazines, radio and television can be trusted to tell the truth about what is going on in the world today—can they be trusted a great deal, some, little, or not at all?

	per cent
A great deal	14.2
Some	54.8
Little	23.1
Not at all	6.2
Don't know	1.6

46. In your opinion, are foreign affairs and military defense so complicated these days that they should be left to the government authorities in Washington, or do you think that people like yourself should have something to say about them?

	per cent
Left to authorities	44.1
People say about them	50.4
Don't know	5.5

47. In your opinion does the military have too much influence or not enough influence on what this country's foreign policy should be?

	per cent
Too much	27.9
Not enough	31.1
About right	22.2
Don't know	18.8

On another topic . . .

48. Some people say that this country has become too materialistic and interested in making money. Others say people are right in wanting to make as much money as they can. What side do you agree with more?

	per cent
Too materialistic	43.6
Right to make money	51.0
Don't know	5.4

49. Some people say that we need to experiment with new ways of dealing with the nation's problems. Others say that there has been too much experimentation already. Which side do you agree with more?

	per cent
Need to experiment	48.4
Too much experimentation	41.6
Don't know	10.1

50. Some people say young people are too critical today about this country. Others say that this criticism is needed and should be kept up. Which side do you agree with more?

	per cent
Young too critical	39.0
Criticism needed	53.9
Don't know	7.1

51. (HAND RESPONDENT CARD F) Which one statement on this card best describes your feelings about the demands being made by Negro leaders these days?

	per cent
These demands are completely justified and should be met right away.	1.3
Most of these demands are justified, but it will take some time to meet them.	12.2
Some of these demands are justified, but it will take some time to meet them.	56.4
Very few of these demands are justified, and they have pretty much been taken care of.	19.0
These demands are completely unjustified and they should not be granted.	7.4

52a. In your opinion have demonstrators on college campuses been dealt with too severely or too leniently?

	per cent		
TOO SEVERELY	ALMOST RIGHT	TOO LENIENTLY	DON'T KNOW
3.3	7.9	84.2	4.6

52b. Have black militants been dealt with too severely or too leniently?

per cent			
TOO SEVERELY	ALMOST RIGHT	TOO LENIENTLY	DON'T KNOW
2.7	5.7	85.1	6.5

53. To what extent do you think the morals of this country are being undermined by the current emphasis on sex and nudity in the movies, theaters, books, and magazines—a greal deal, some, a little, or not at all?

	per cent
A great deal	62.2
Some	23.6
A little	8.5
Not at all	4.6
Don't know	1.1

54. What do you think is more important for a young person to do today—get an education that trains him for a job that pays well, or do what he really wants to do even if it means he will never make much money?

	per cent
Education, job	47.2
Whatever wants to do	50.2
Don't know	2.5

55. How good a job do you think the government is doing in solving the problems people like yourself and your family have to face—an excellent job, a good job, a fair job, or a poor job?

	per cent
Excellent job	1.6
Good job	22.4
Fair job	49.8
Poor job	17.2
Don't know	8.9

APPENDIX B:

DESIGN OF THE SAMPLE

The regular Gallup national probability sample of interviewing areas was used in this study with the exception that those areas which were known to be predominantly non-white were excluded from the sample. The design of the Gallup national probability sample is that of a replicated probability sample down to the block level in the case of urban areas, and to segments of townships in the case of rural areas.

After stratifying the nation geographically and by size of community in order to insure conformity of the sample with the latest available estimate of the Census Bureau of the distribution of the adult population, sampling locations or areas were selected on a strictly random basis. The interviewers had no choice whatsoever concerning the part of the city or county in which they conducted their interviews.

Interviewers were given maps of the area to which they were assigned, with a starting point indicated, and required to follow a specified direction. At each dwelling unit occupied by whites, interviewers were instructed to select respondents by following a prescribed systematic method and by a male-female assignment. This procedure was followed until the assigned number of interviews was completed.

Since this sampling procedure is designed to produce a sample which approximates the adult white civilian population (21 and older) living in private households in the United States (that is, excluding those in prisons and hospitals, hotels, religious and educational institutions, and on military reservations), the survey results can be applied to this population for the purpose of projecting percentages into number of people.

COMPOSITION OF THE SAMPLE

	per cent
National	100.0
Sex	
Men	47.7
Women	52.3
	100.0
Age of Respondent	
Under 30 years	21.9
30–54 years	45.9
55 years and older	31.8
Undesignated	.4
	100.0
Annual Family Income	
$15,000 and over	13.6
$5,000–$14,999	60.4
Under $5,000	24.5
Undesignated	1.5
	100.0
Education	
College or university	25.3
High school	52.8
Grade school	21.8
Undesignated	.1
	100.0
Occupation of Chief Wage Earner	
Professional & Business: Professional, technical and kindred workers (e.g., engineers, accountants, nurses); Executives (e.g., managers, officials, proprietors, public administrators)	28.0
Clerical & Sales: Clerical and kindred workers (e.g., mail carriers, telephone operators); Sales and kindred workers (e.g., retail clerks, claims examiners)	9.1

Manual Workers: Foremen, craftsmen and kindred workers (e.g., railroad engineers, machinists, linesmen, maintenance painters); Operatives and kindred workers (e.g., coal miners, truck drivers, butchers, apprentices); Service workers, Laborers	38.8
Farmers: Farm owners, farm managers, farm foremen, farm laborers	6.5
Non-labor force	16.1
Undesignated	1.5
	100.0

Region of the Country

East:	Maine, New Hampshire, Rhode Island, Connecticut, Vermont, Massachusetts, New York, New Jersey, Pennsylvania, West Virginia, Delaware, Maryland, District of Columbia	26.3
Midwest:	Ohio, Indiana, Illinois, Michigan, Minnesota, Wisconsin, Iowa, North Dakota, South Dakota, Kansas, Nebraska, Missouri	29.4
South:	Kentucky, Tennessee, Virginia, North Carolina, South Carolina, Georgia, Florida, Alabama, Mississippi, Texas, Arkansas, Oklahoma, Louisiana	28.1
West:	Arizona, New Mexico, Colorado, Nevada, Montana, Idaho, Wyoming, Utah, California, Washington, Oregon, Alaska, Hawaii	16.2
		100.0

Size of Community

Central City	27.0
Suburbs	25.7
2,500–49,999	15.6
Under 2,500	31.7
	100.0

Religion

Protestant	63.6
Roman Catholic	27.4
Jewish	2.9
All other	6.1
	100.0

Adults in Household*

One	12.1
Two	71.7
Three	11.7
Four	3.3
Five or more	.6
Undesignated	.6
	100.0

*21 years of age or older

Home Ownership

Own	69.4
Rent	26.8
Other arrangement	3.4
Undesignated	.4
	100.0

Labor Union Membership

Respondent	13.6
Spouse	9.0
Respondent and spouse	1.7
Neither	73.5
Undesignated	2.2
	100.0

Political Party Identification

Republican	27.5
Democrat	36.0
Independent	33.5
All other	3.0
	100.0

Voted for in 1968 Election

Nixon	38.6
Humphrey	25.0
Wallace	9.3
Other	.6
Voted, don't remember for whom	1.5
Didn't vote	22.5
Don't remember	1.5
Undesignated	1.0
	100.0

NOTE

Allowance for persons not at home was made by means of a "times-at-home" technique rather than by "call-backs." Either procedure is a standard method for reducing the sample bias that would otherwise result from under-representation in the sample of persons who are difficult to find at home. All results reported including the composition of the sample are based on data in which a "times-at-home" weighting has been incorporated. The actual number of interviews made for various population groups are reported in the findings.

APPENDIX C:

SAMPLING TOLERANCES

In interpreting survey results, it should be borne in mind that all sample surveys are subject to sampling error—that is, the extent to which the results may differ from what would be obtained if the whole population surveyed had been interviewed. The size of such sampling errors depends largely on the number of interviews.

The following tables may be used in estimating the sampling error of any percentage in this report. The computed allowances have taken into account the effect of the sample design upon sampling errors. They may be interpreted as indicating the range (plus or minus the figure shown) within which the results of repeated samplings in the same time period could be expected to vary, 95 per cent of the time, assuming the same sampling procedure, the same interviewers, and the same questionnaire.

The first table shows how much allowance should be made for the sampling error of a percentage:

RECOMMENDED ALLOWANCE FOR
SAMPLING ERROR OF A PERCENTAGE

	In Percentage Points (at 95 in 100 confidence level)*							
	SAMPLE SIZE							
	2200	1500	1000	750	600	400	200	100
Percentages near 10	2	2	2	3	3	4	5	7
Percentages near 20	2	2	3	4	4	5	7	9
Percentages near 30	3	3	4	4	4	6	8	10
Percentages near 40	3	3	4	4	5	6	8	11
Percentages near 50	3	3	4	4	5	6	8	11
Percentages near 60	3	3	4	4	5	6	8	11
Percentages near 70	3	3	4	4	4	6	8	10
Percentages near 80	2	2	3	4	4	5	7	9
Percentages near 90	2	2	2	3	3	4	5	7

The table would be used in the following manner: Let us say a reported percentage is 33 for a group which includes 1500 respondents. Then we go to row "percentages near 30" in the table and go across to the column headed "1500." The number at this point is 3, which means that the 33 per cent obtained in the sample is subject to a sampling error of plus or minus 3 points. Another way of saying it is that very probably (95 chances out of 100) the average of repeated samplings would be somewhere between 30 and 36, with the most likely figure the 33 obtained.

In comparing survey results in two samples, such as, for example, men and women, the question arises as to how large must a difference between them be before one can be reasonably sure that it reflects a real difference. In the tables below, the number of points which must be allowed for in such comparisons is indicated.

Two tables are provided. One is for percentages near 20 or 80; the other for percentages near 50. For percentages in between, the error to be allowed for is between that shown in the two tables:

---

*The chances are 95 in 100 that the sampling error is not larger than the figures shown.

RECOMMENDED ALLOWANCE FOR
SAMPLING ERROR OF THE DIFFERENCE

. *In Percentage Points (at 95
in 100 confidence level)**

TABLE A *Percentages near 20 or percentages near 80*

Size of Sample	1100	750	600	400	200
1100	4				
750	5	5			
600	5	5	6		
400	6	6	6	7	
200	8	8	8	8	10

TABLE B *Percentages near 50*

Size of Sample	1100	750	600	400	200
1100	6				
750	6	6			
600	7	7	7		
400	8	7	8	8	
200	10	10	10	10	12

Here is an example of how the tables would be used: Let us say that 50 per cent of men respond a certain way and 40 per cent of women respond that way also, for a difference of 10 percentage points between them. Can we say with any assurance that the 10-point difference reflects a real difference between men and women on the question? The sample contains approximately 1100 men and 1100 women.

Since the percentages are near 50, we consult Table B, and since the two samples are about 1100 persons each, we look for the number in the column headed "1100" which is also in the row designated "1100." We find the number 6 here. This means that the allowance for error should be 6 points, and that in concluding that the percentage among men is somewhere between 4 and 16 points higher than the percentage among women, we should be wrong only about 5 per cent of the time. In other words, we can conclude with considerable confidence that a difference exists in the direction observed and that it amounts to at least 4 percentage points.

---

*The chances are 95 in 100 that the sampling error is not larger than the figures shown.

If, in another case, men's responses amount to 22 per cent, say, and women's 24 per cent, we consult Table A because these percentages are near 20. We look in the column headed "1100" and see that the number is 4. Obviously, then, the 2-point difference is inconclusive.

INDEX